Dances of the World

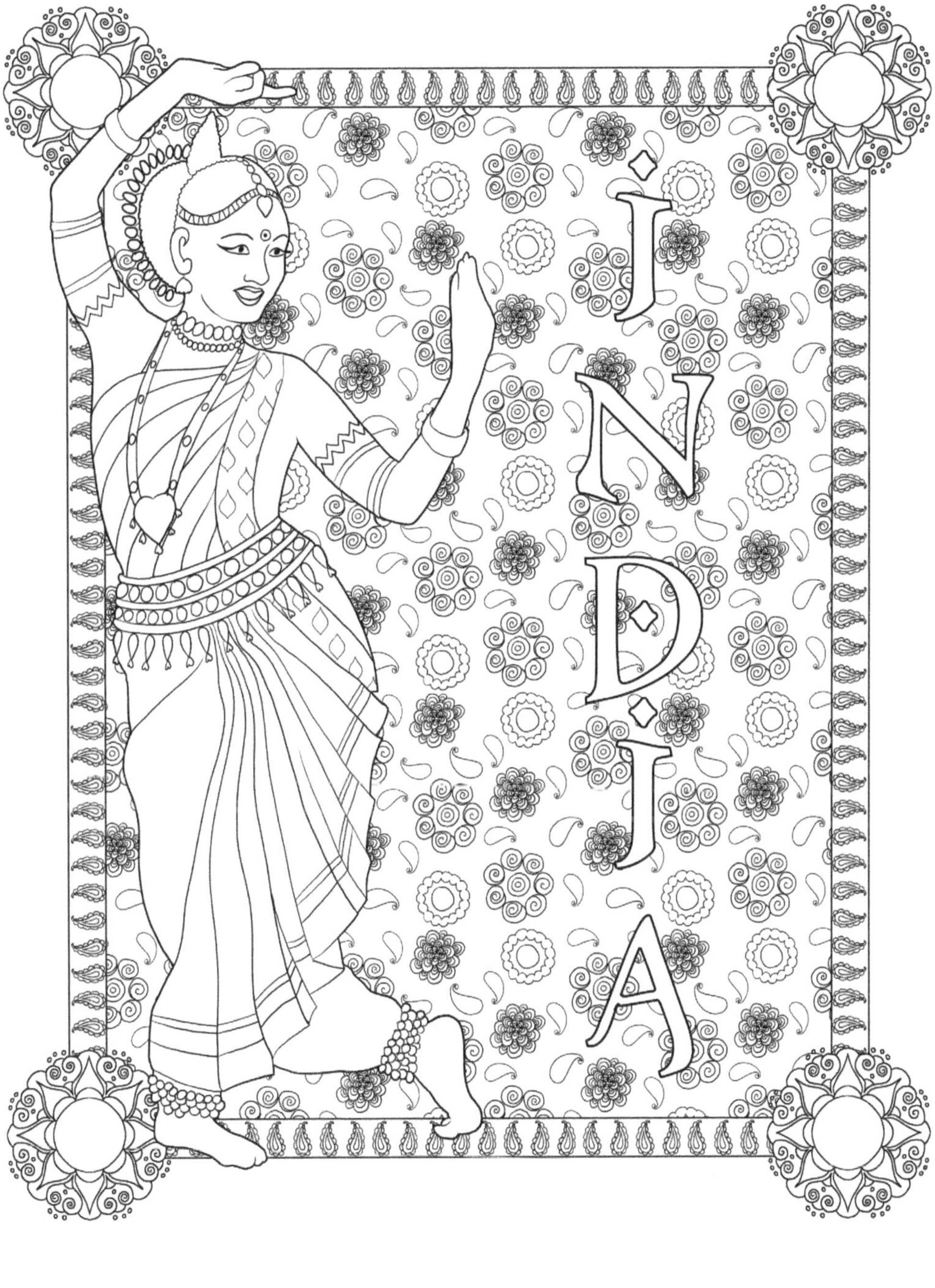

INDIA

Introduction

The 36 drawings that Laura Anne Passarello created for this book depict dances from many of the countries around the world. Her exceptional artistic ability is obvious in these nuanced and elegant illustrations spanning the diverse civilizations. Dance has been and continues to be a major aspect of a culture's rites, rituals and social activities.

The book contains three sections with each covering a different region of the world. Each section contains 12 different dances from 12 different countries. The three major geographies are:

1) The Americas
2) Europe
3) Asia/Pacific

You will find creativity-stimulating images of dances known throughout the world such as the tango of Argentina, the step dance of Ireland and the belly dance of Turkey. And, you will find lesser-known exotic dances such as the jaran kepang of Suriname, the kolo of Serbia and the aspara of Cambodia.

This book is your passport for a virtual journey around the world. Its illustrations reflect the great cultural diversity that exists on our planet. Dance is used to express beauty, joy, love, reverence and a wide variety of other emotions.

THE AMERICAS

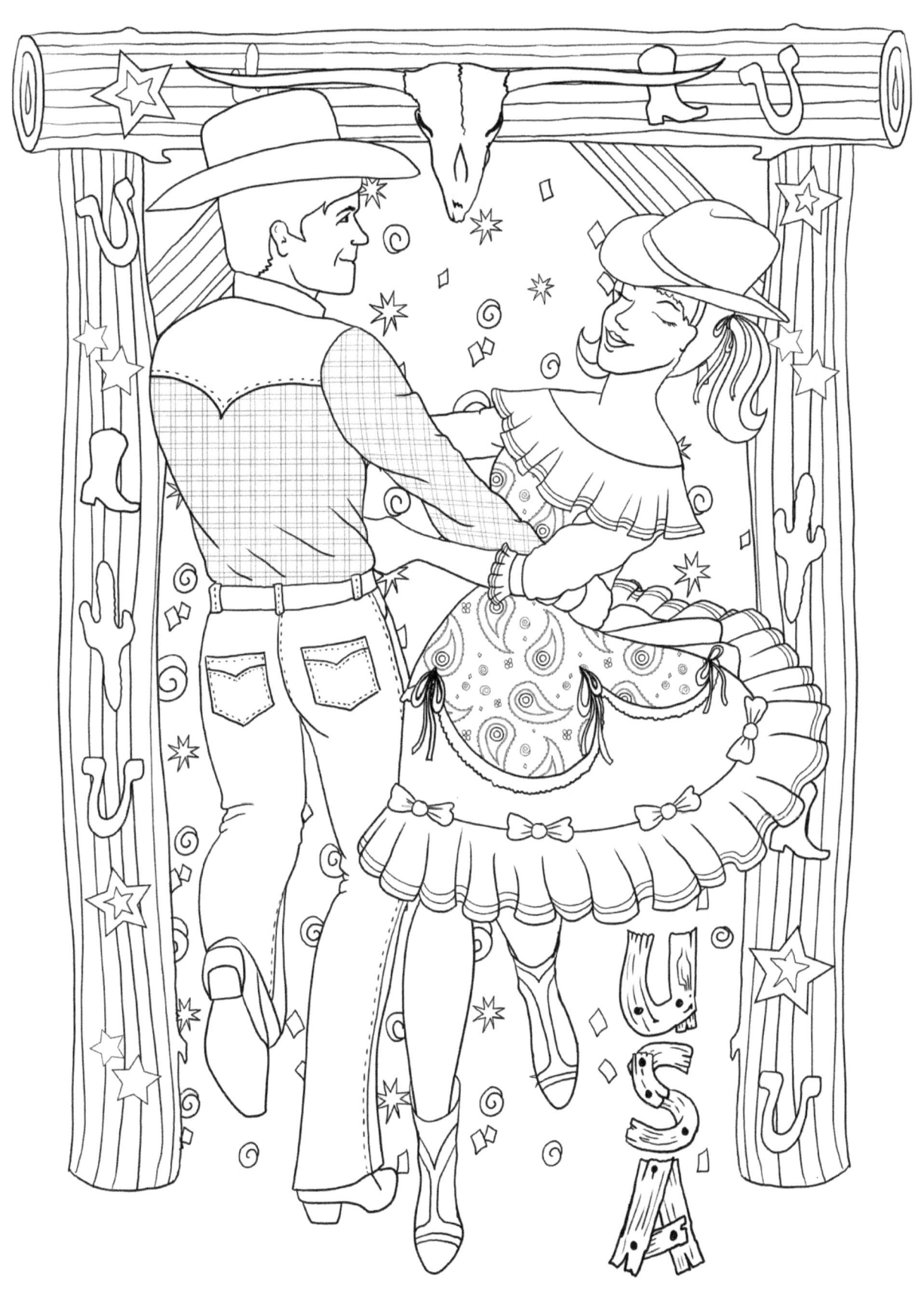

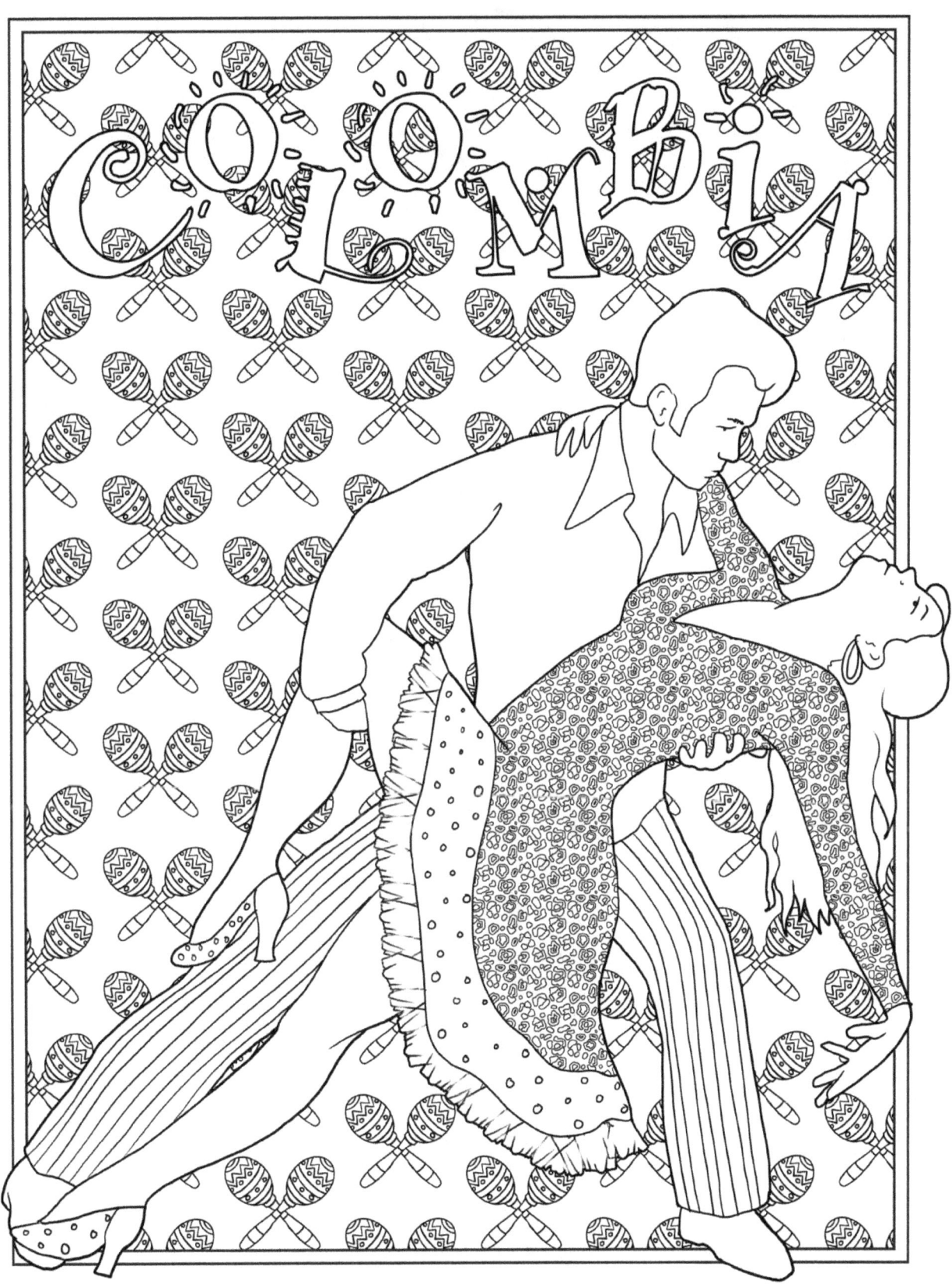

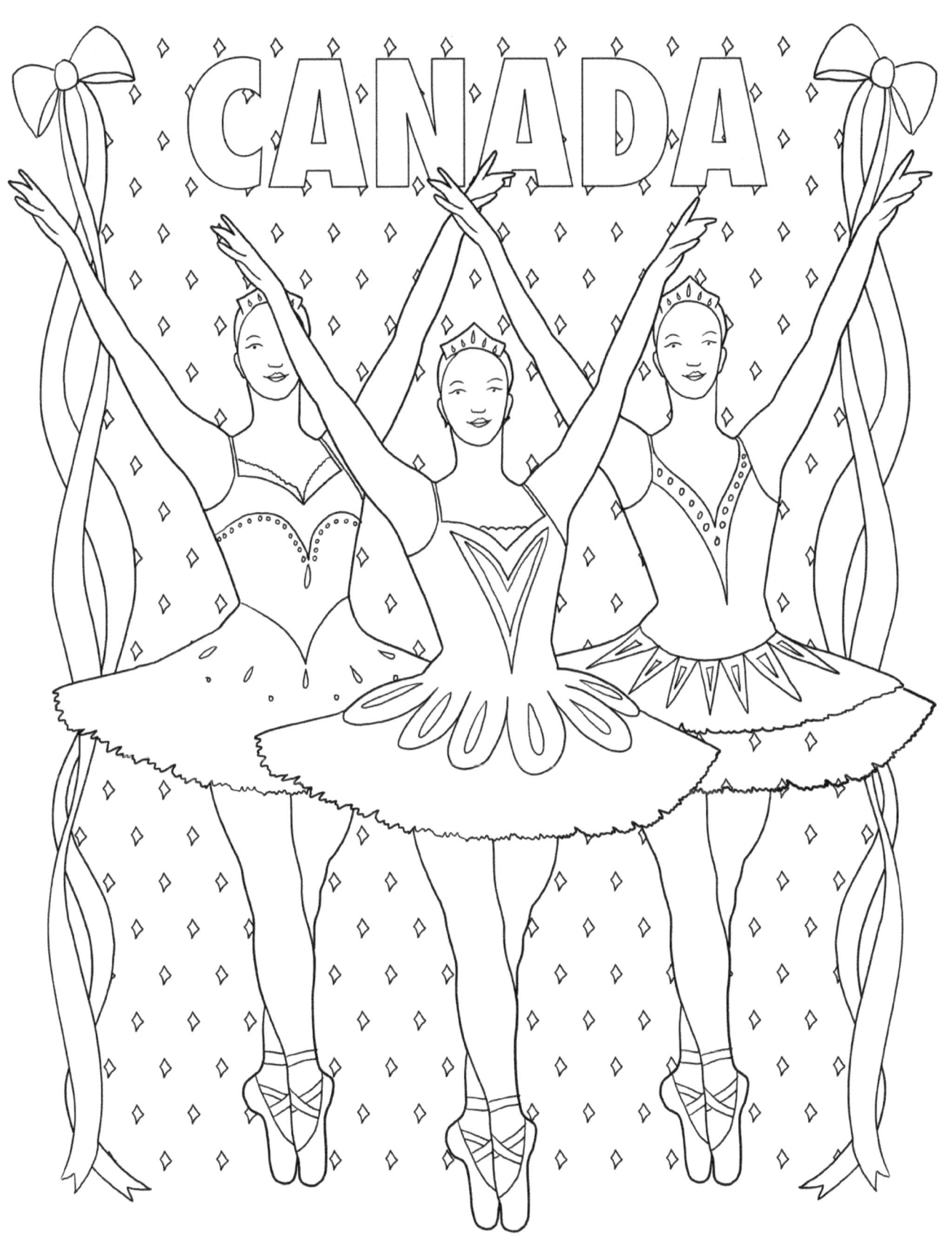

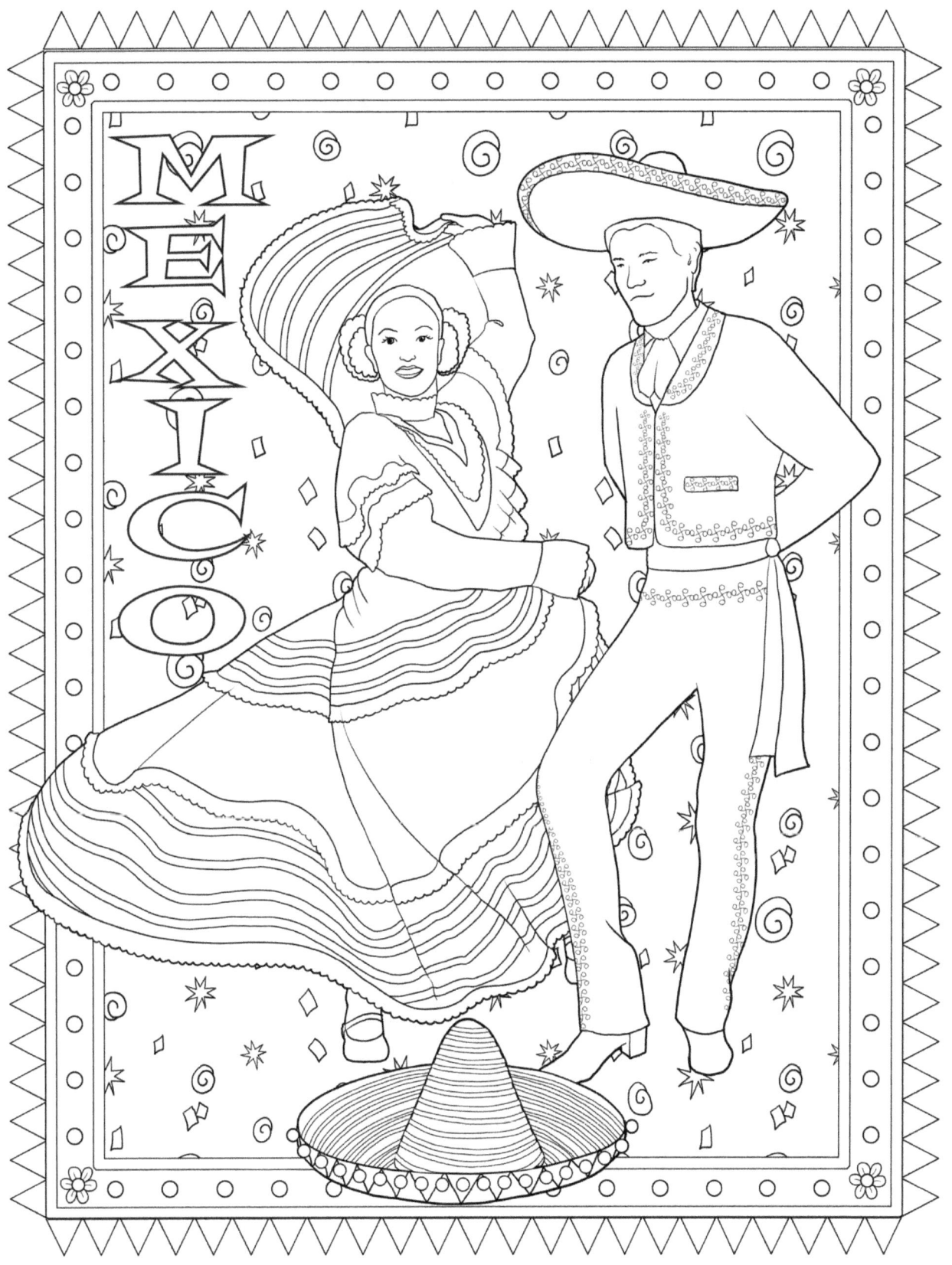

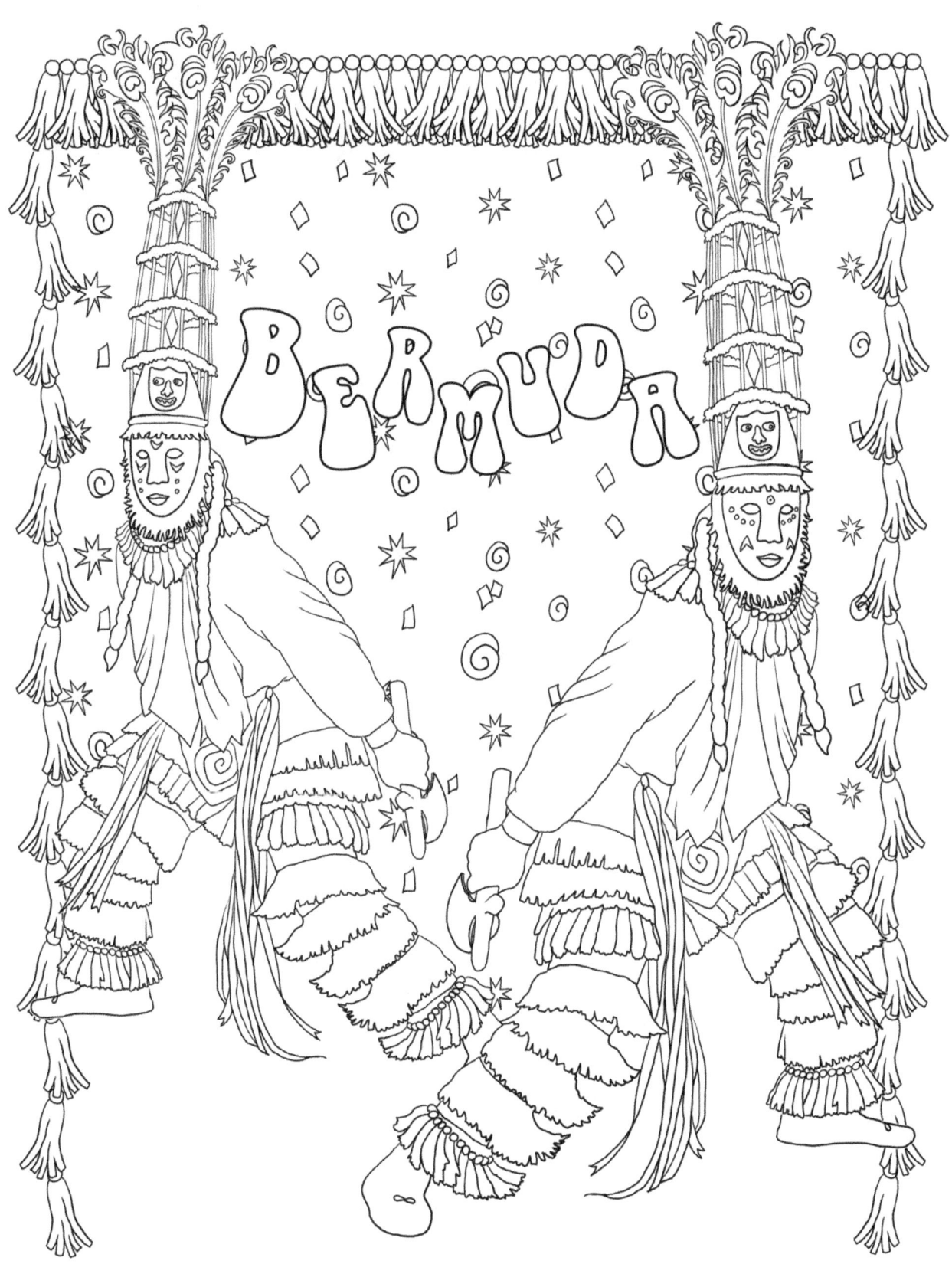

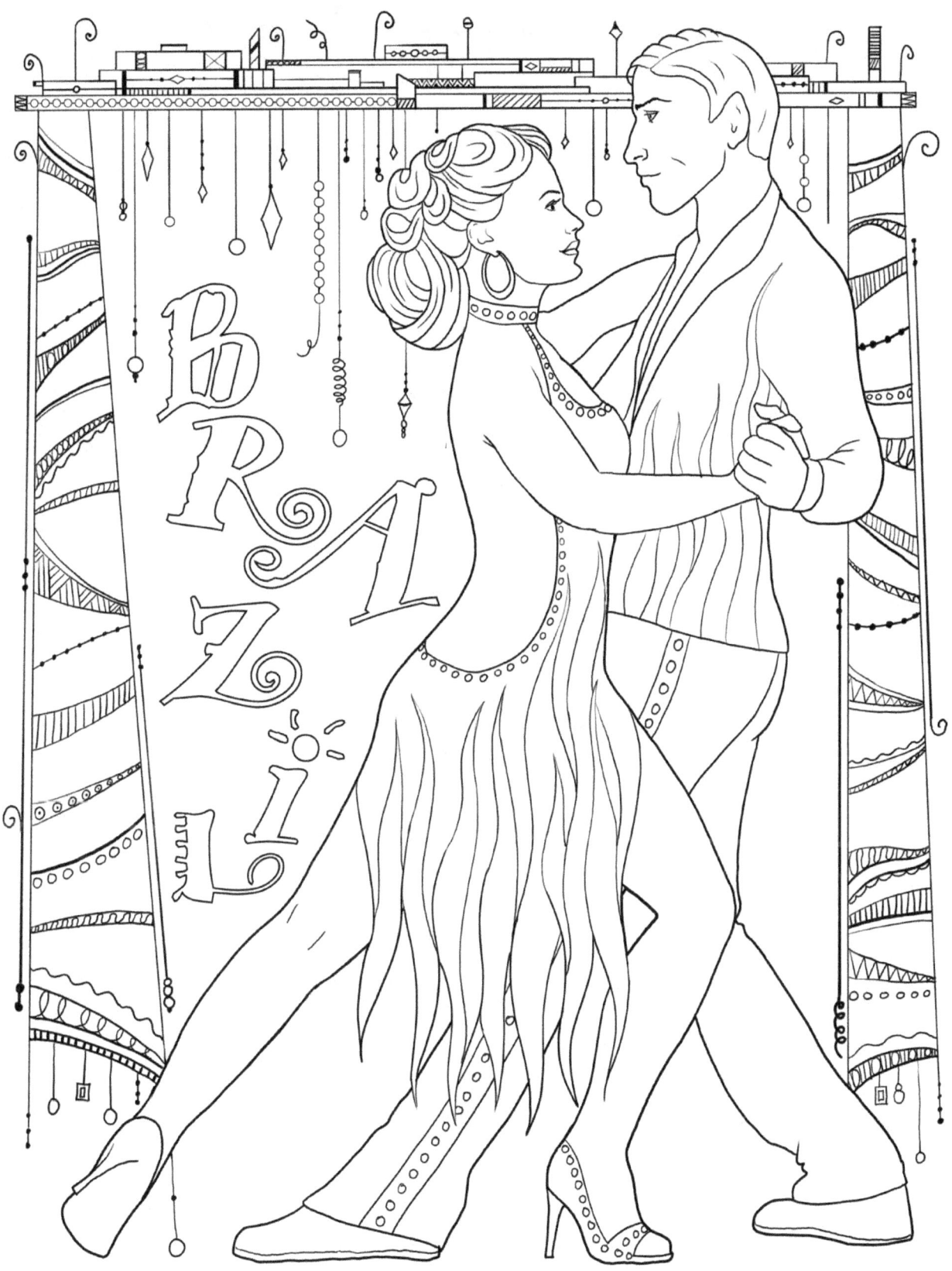

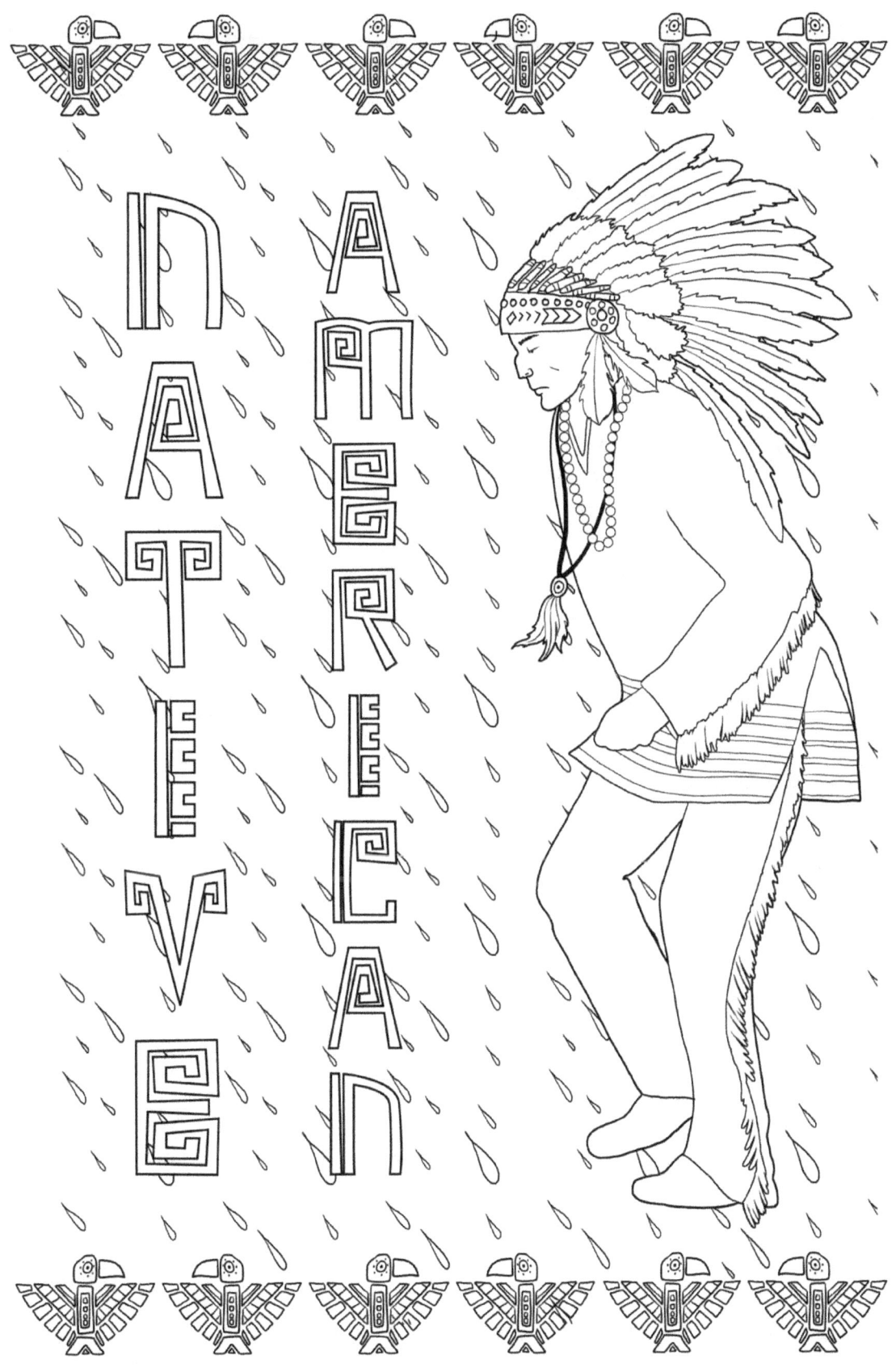

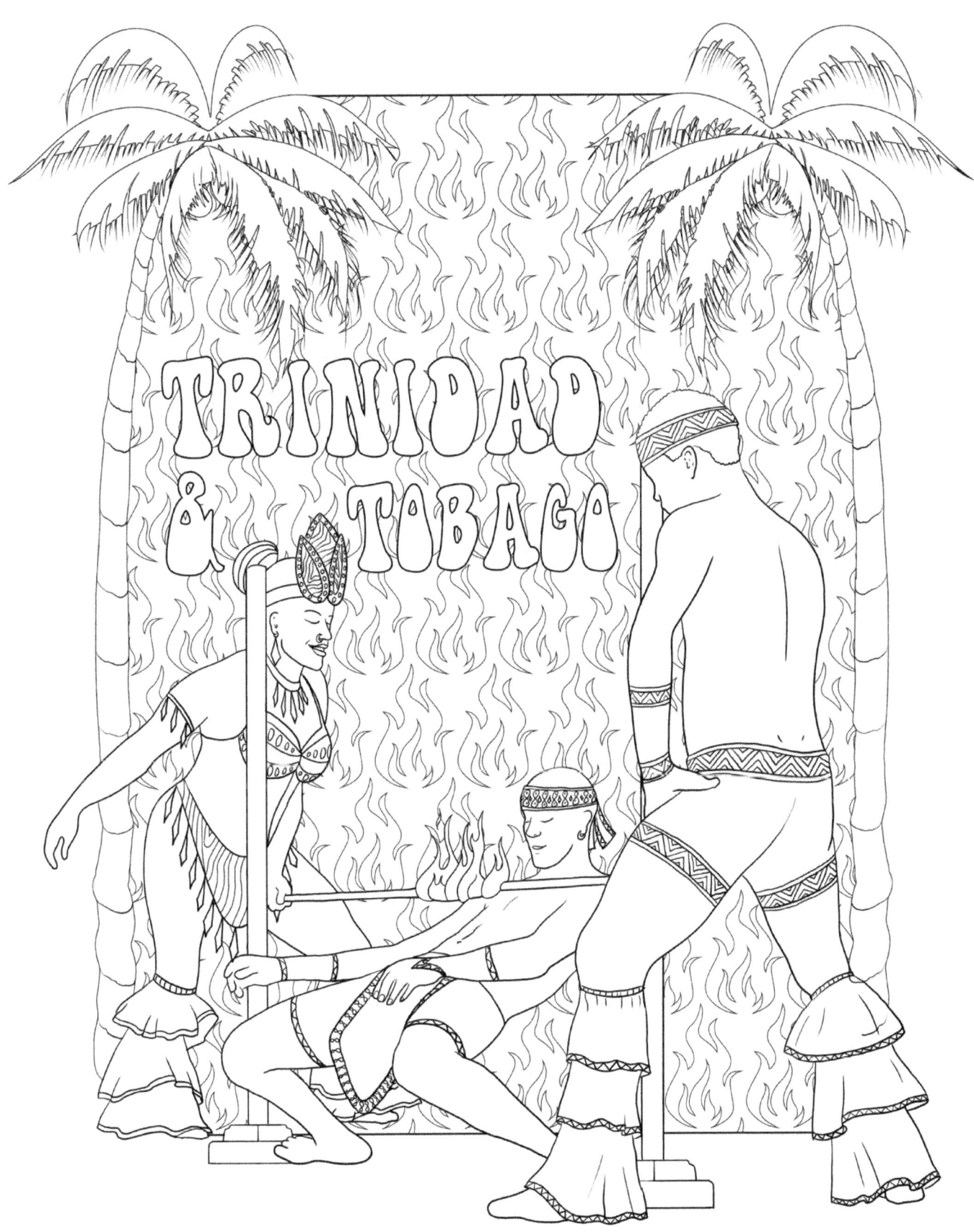

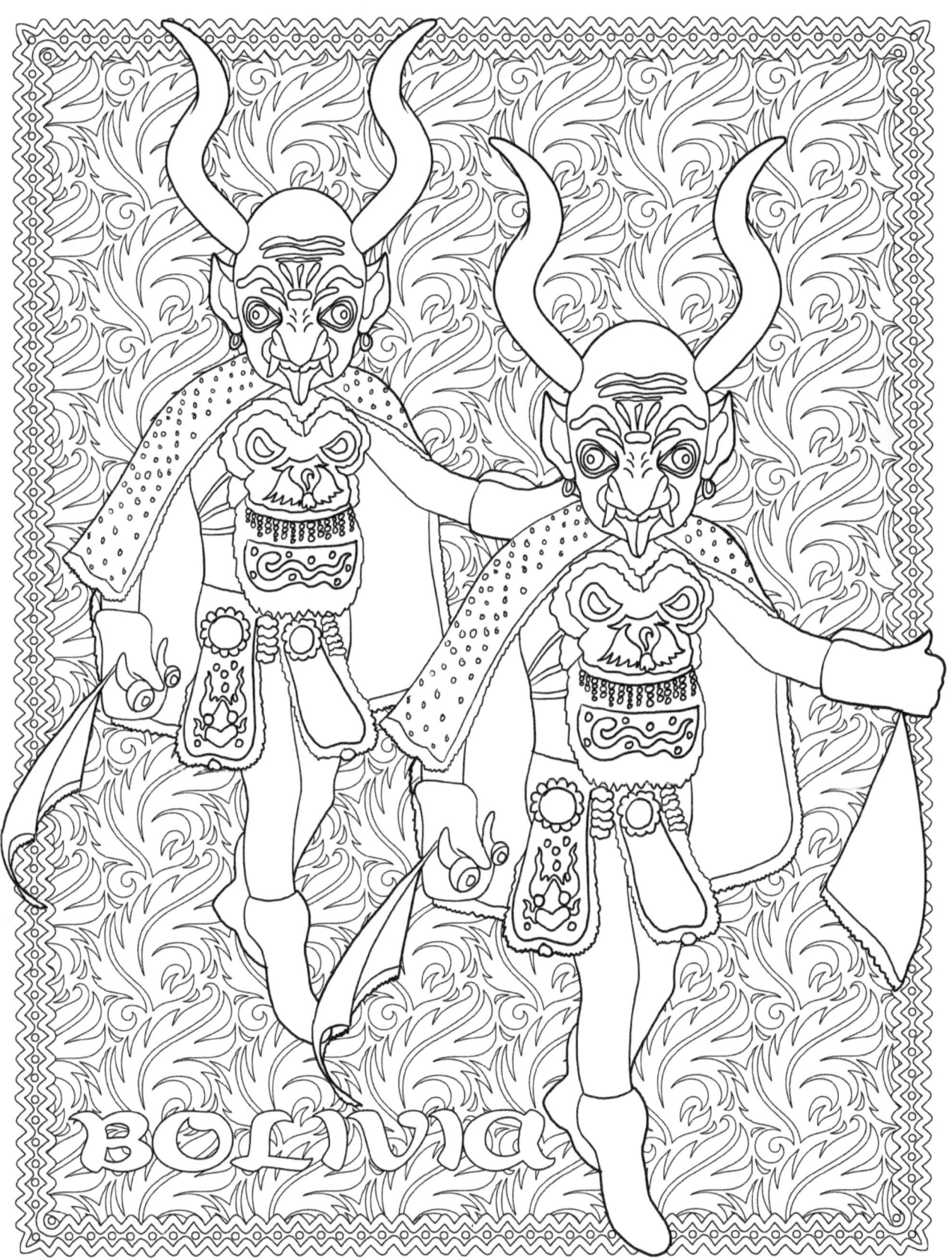

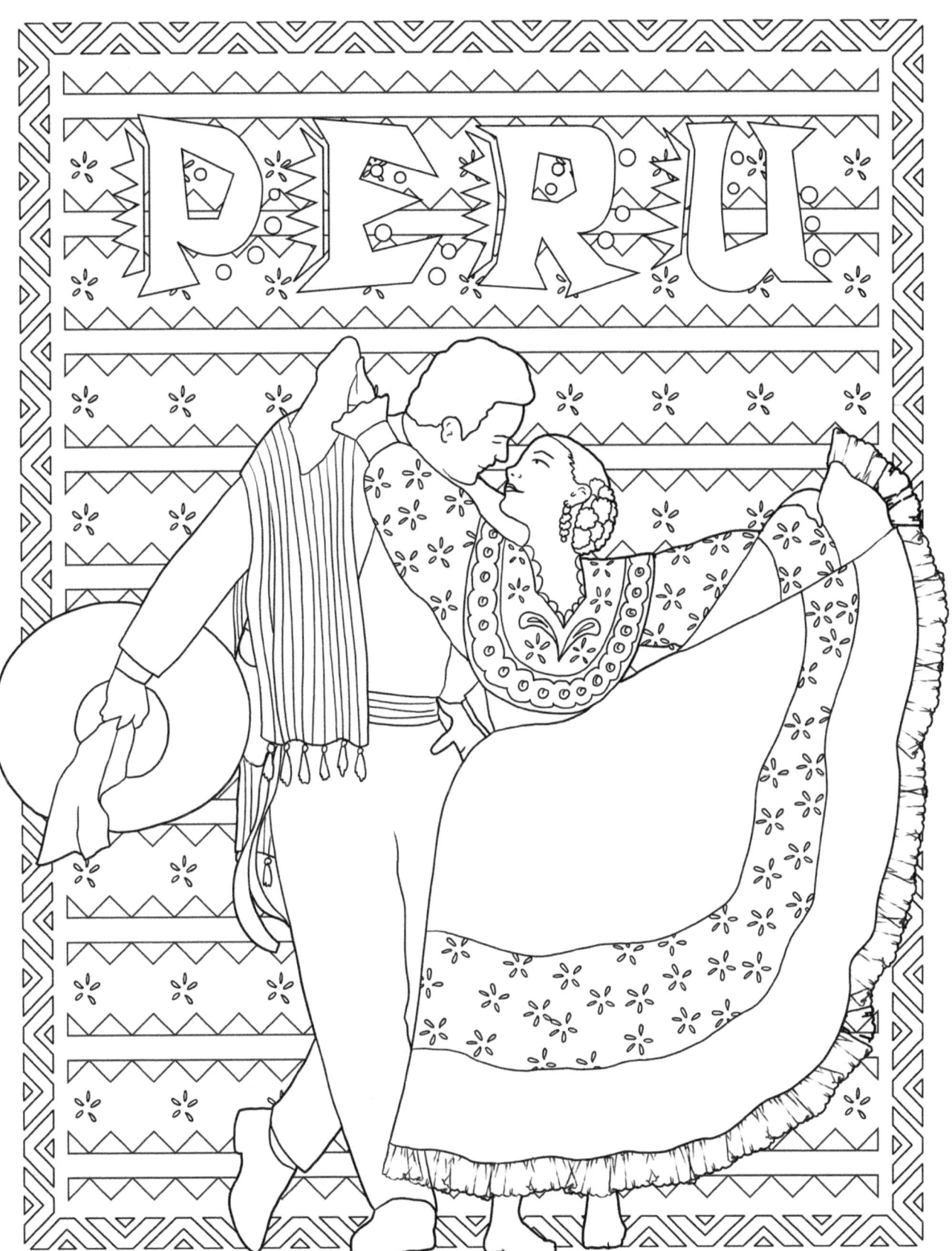

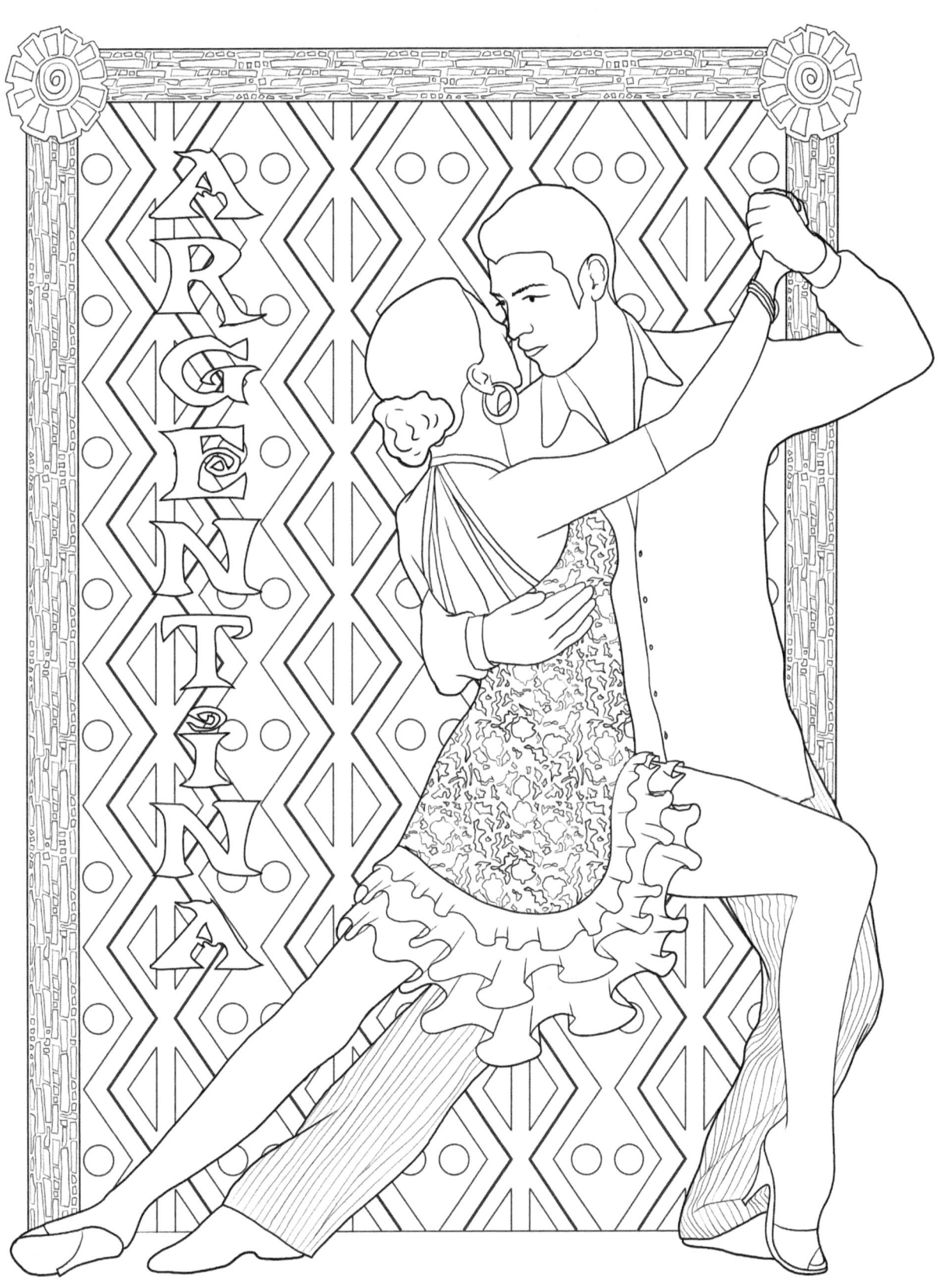

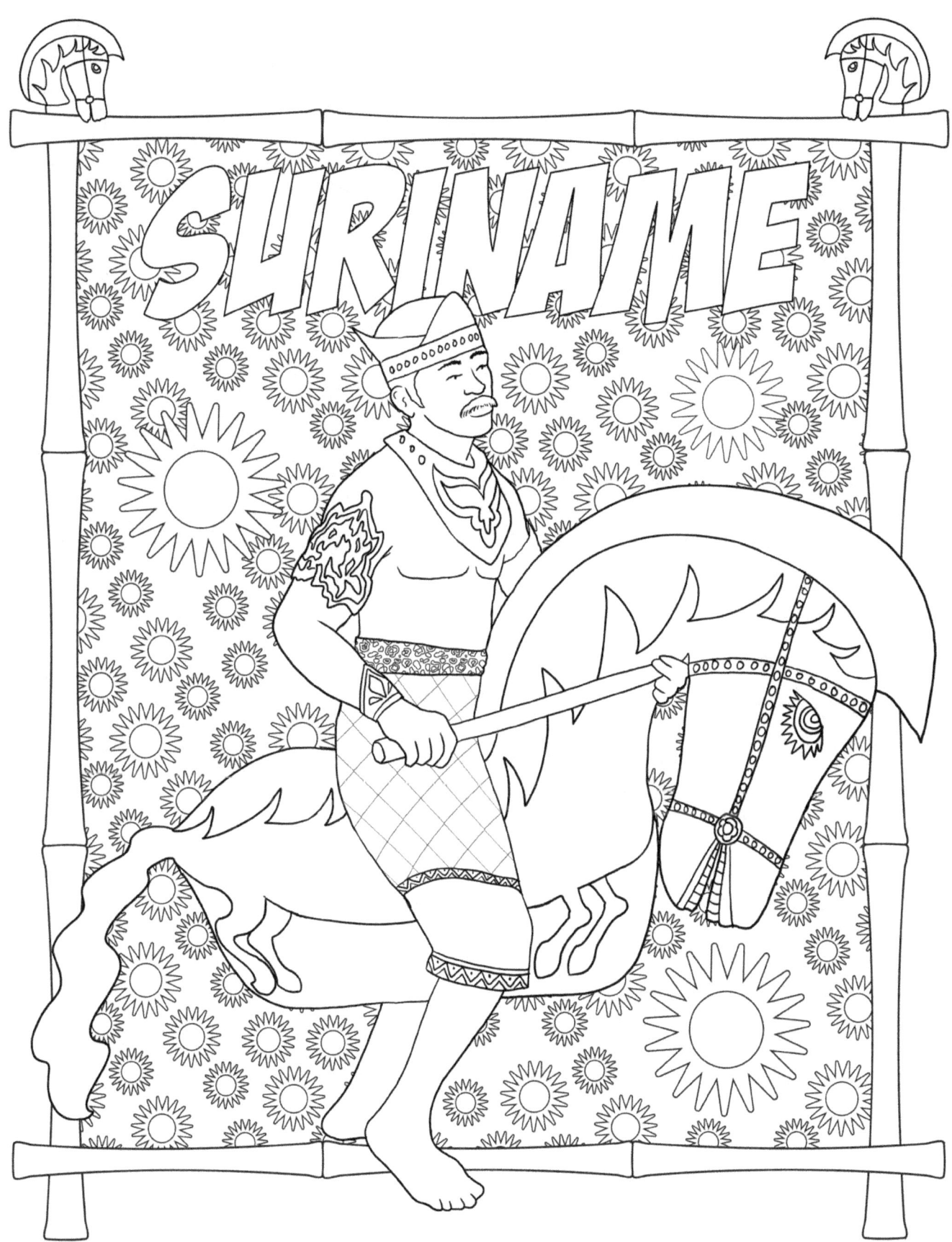

EUROPE

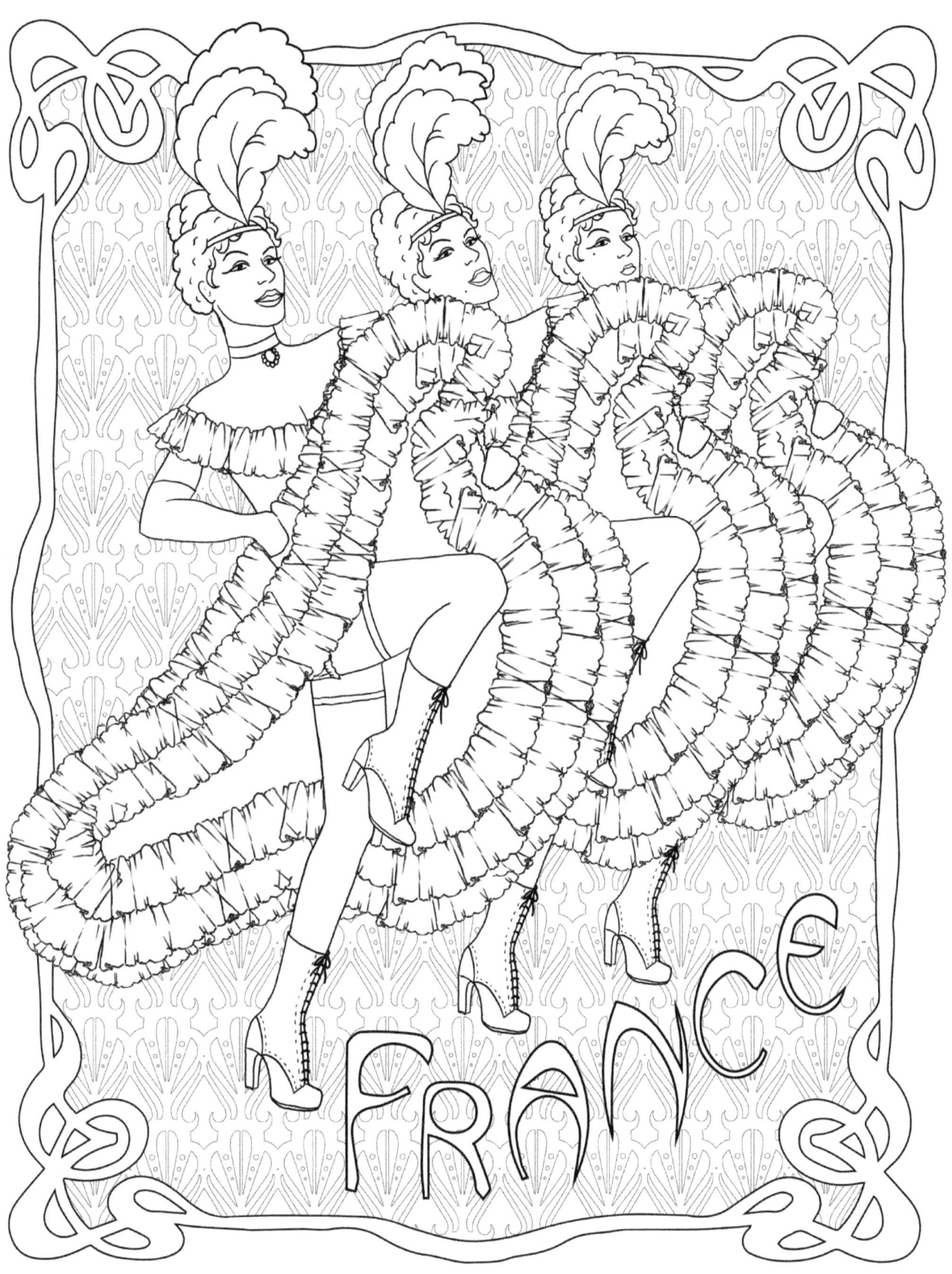

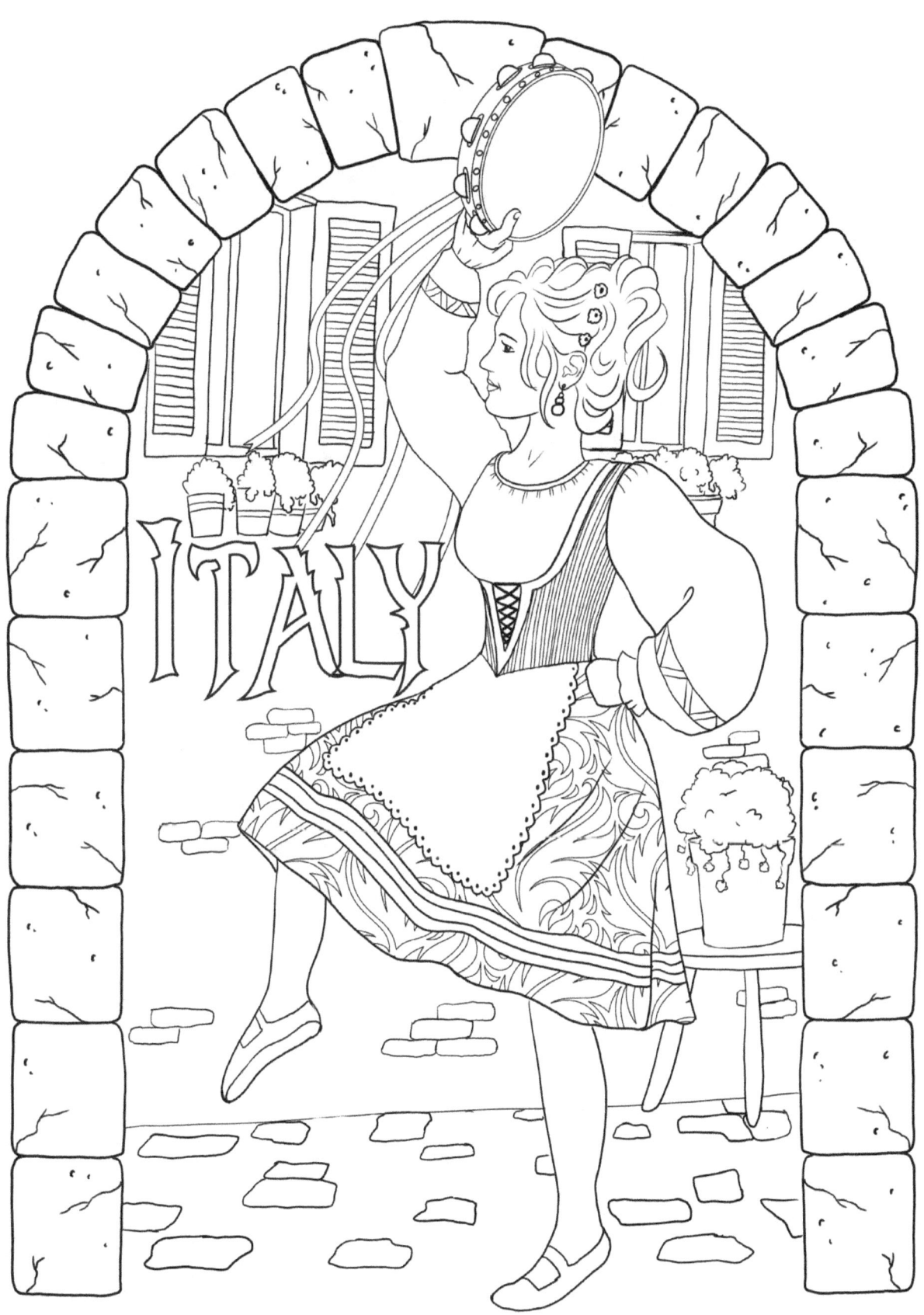

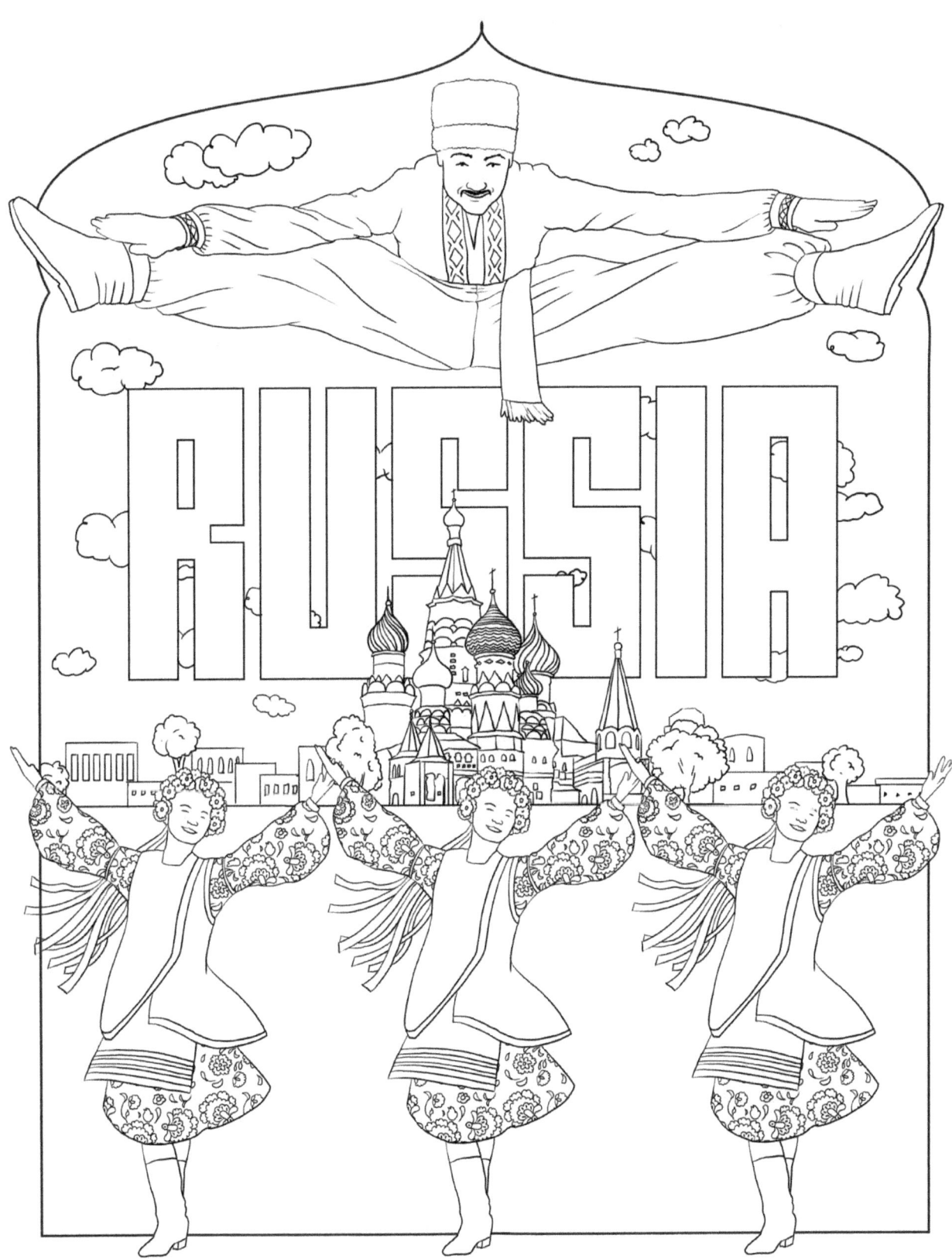

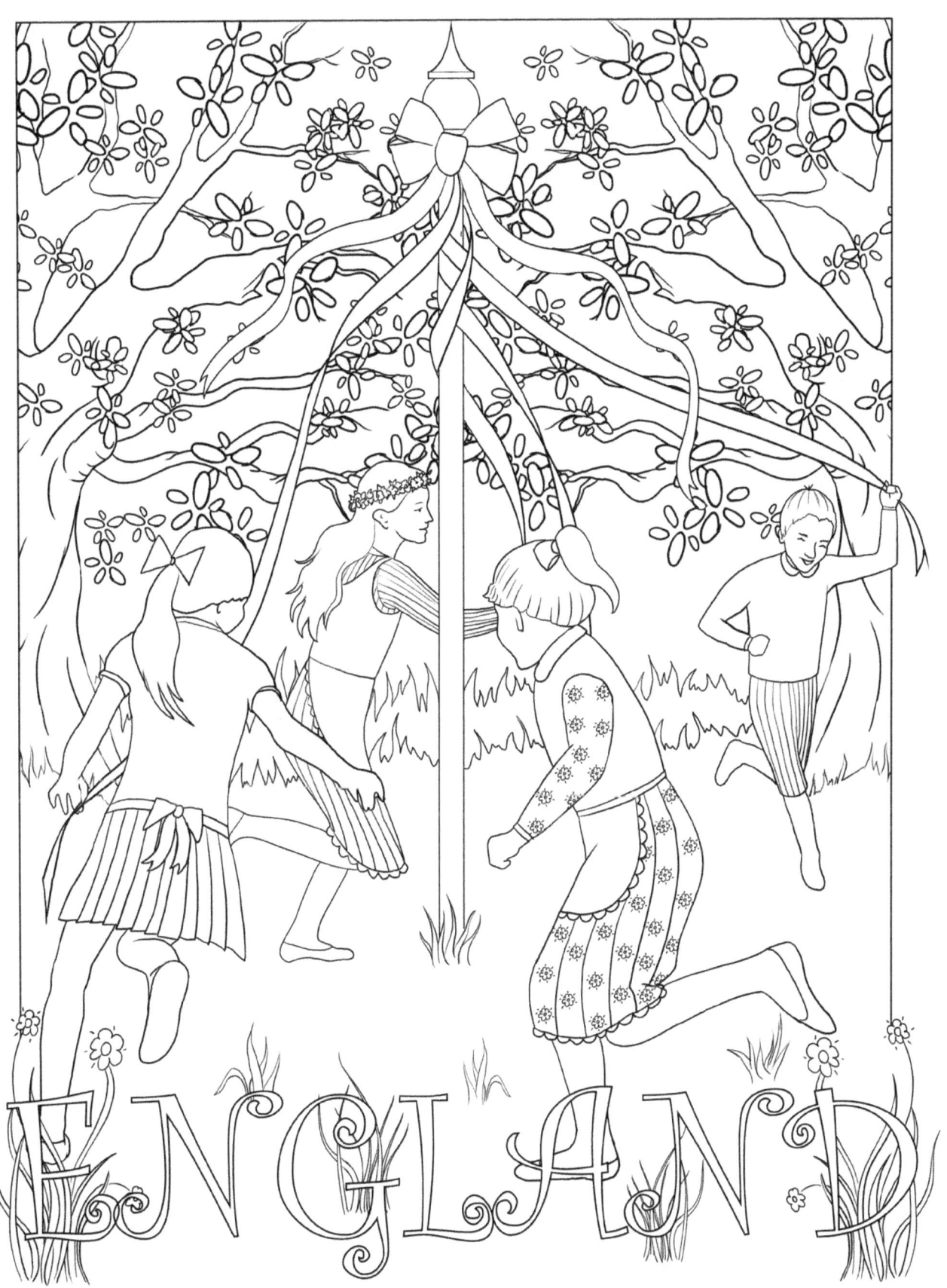

ENGLAND

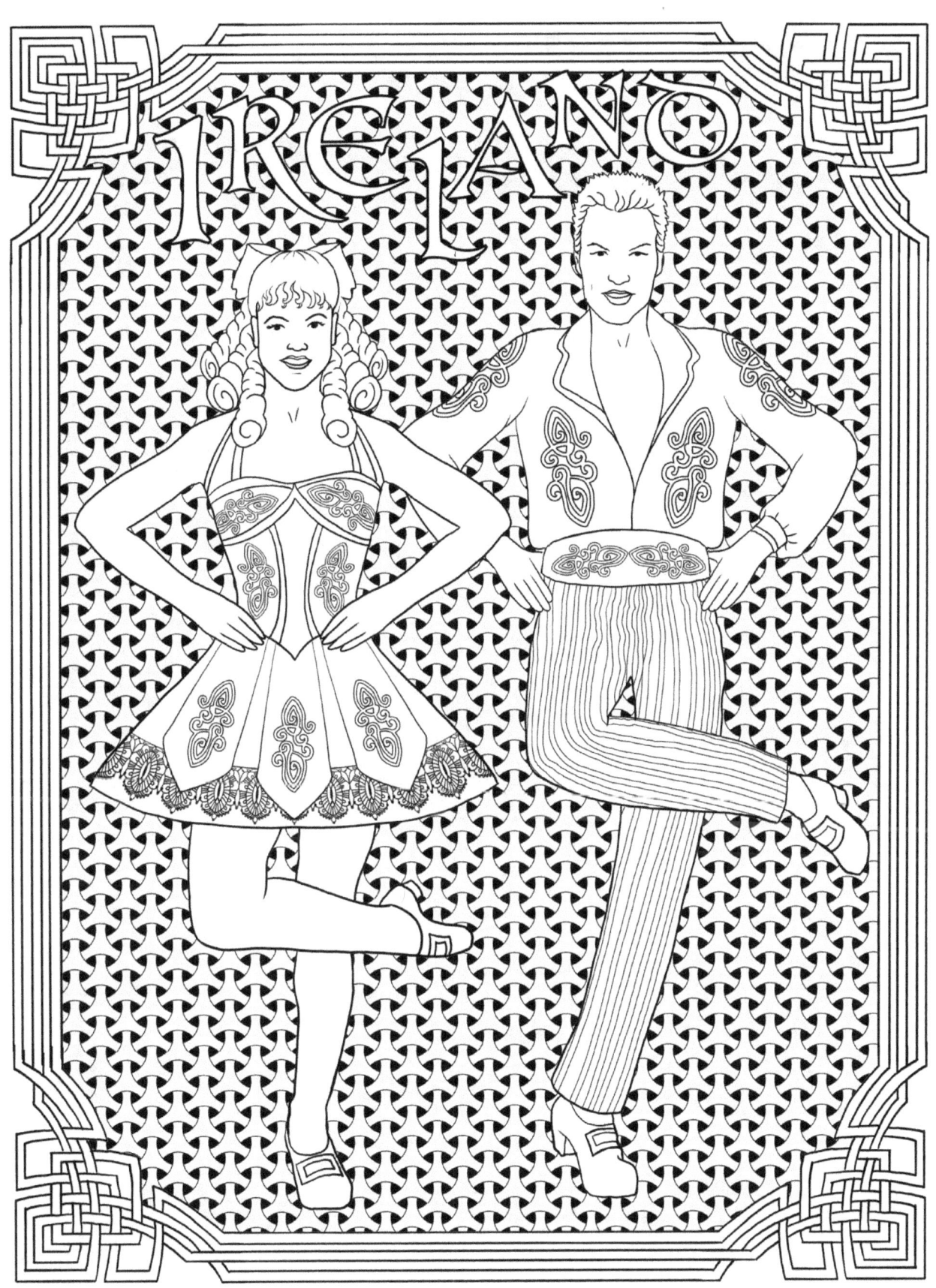

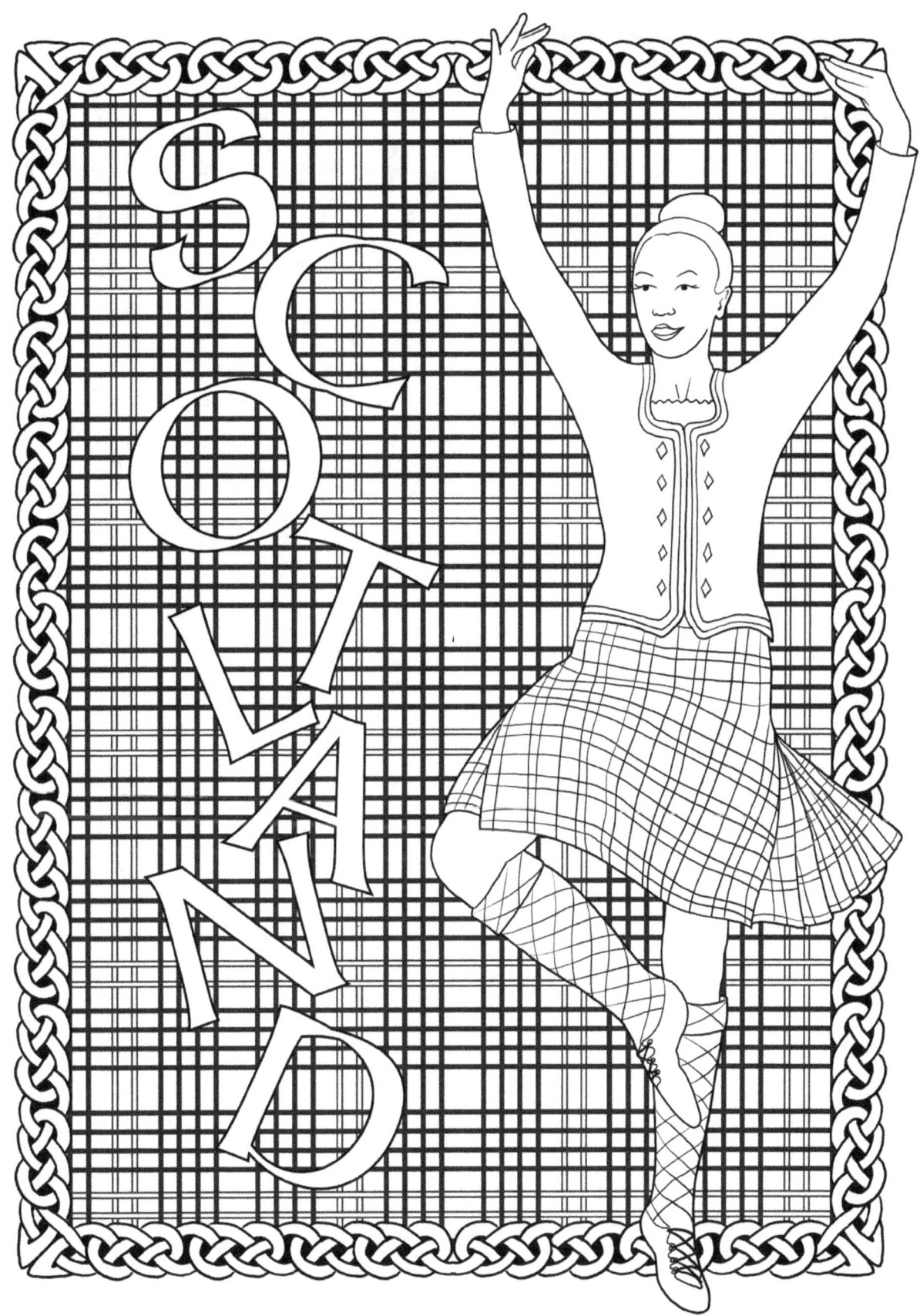

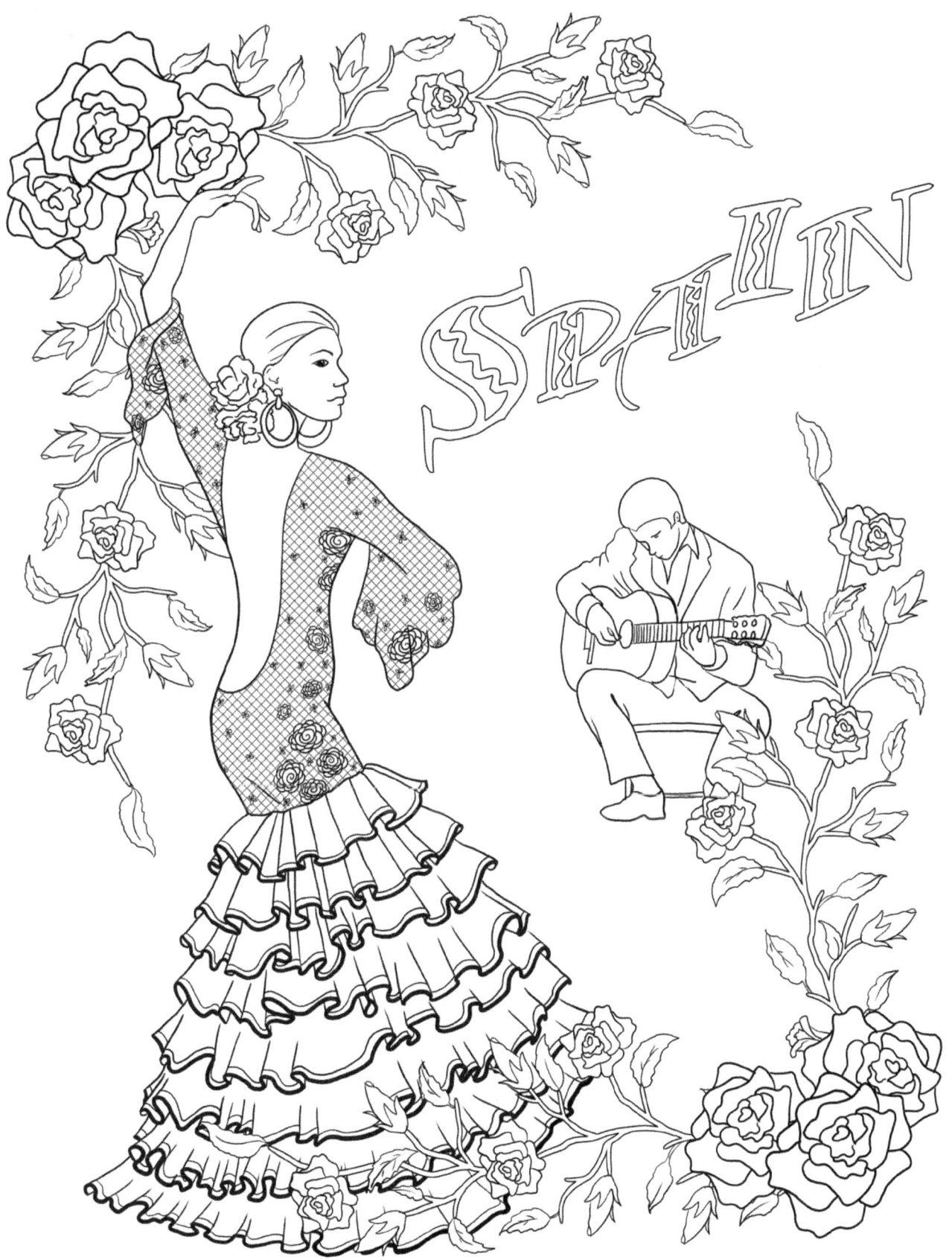

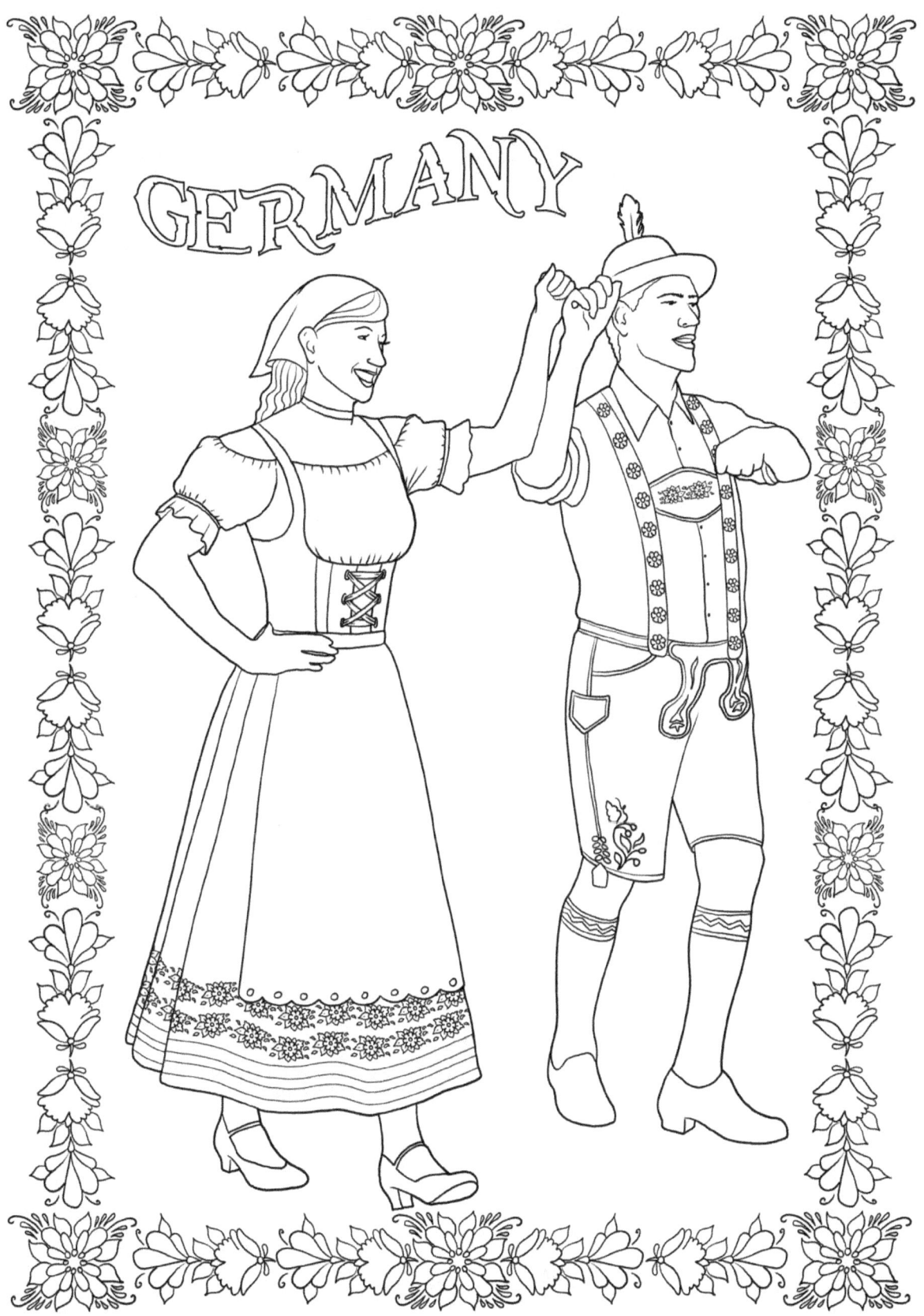

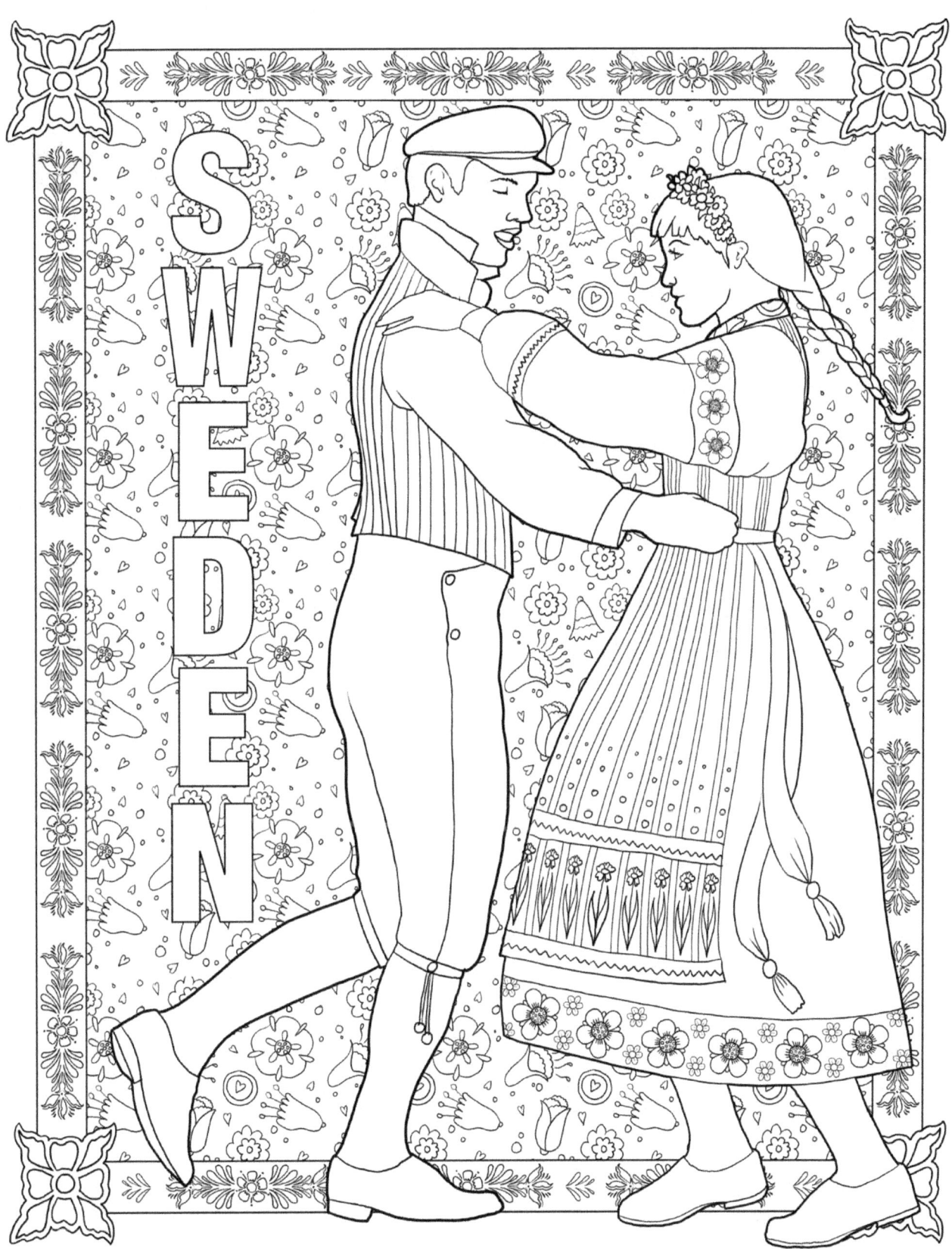

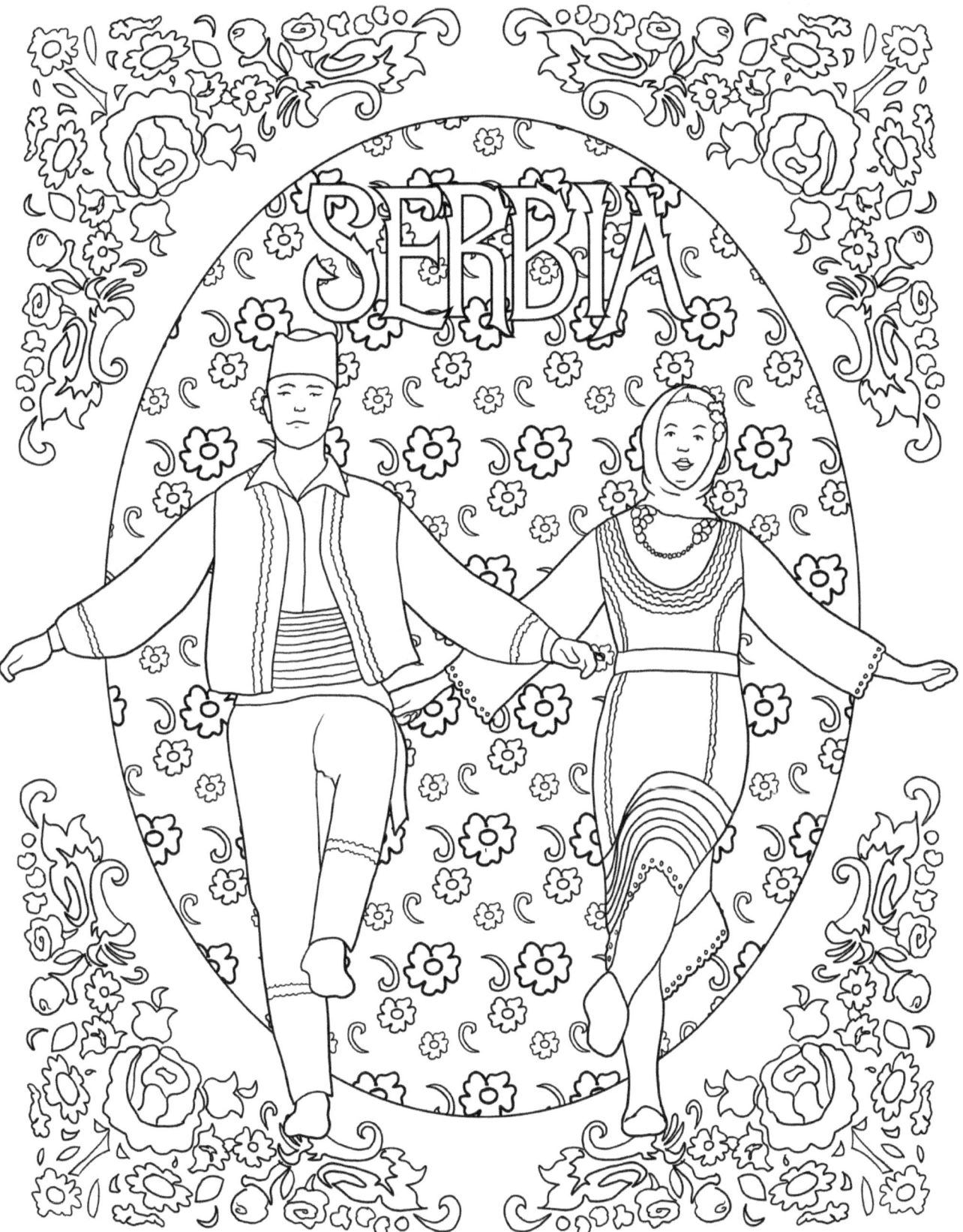

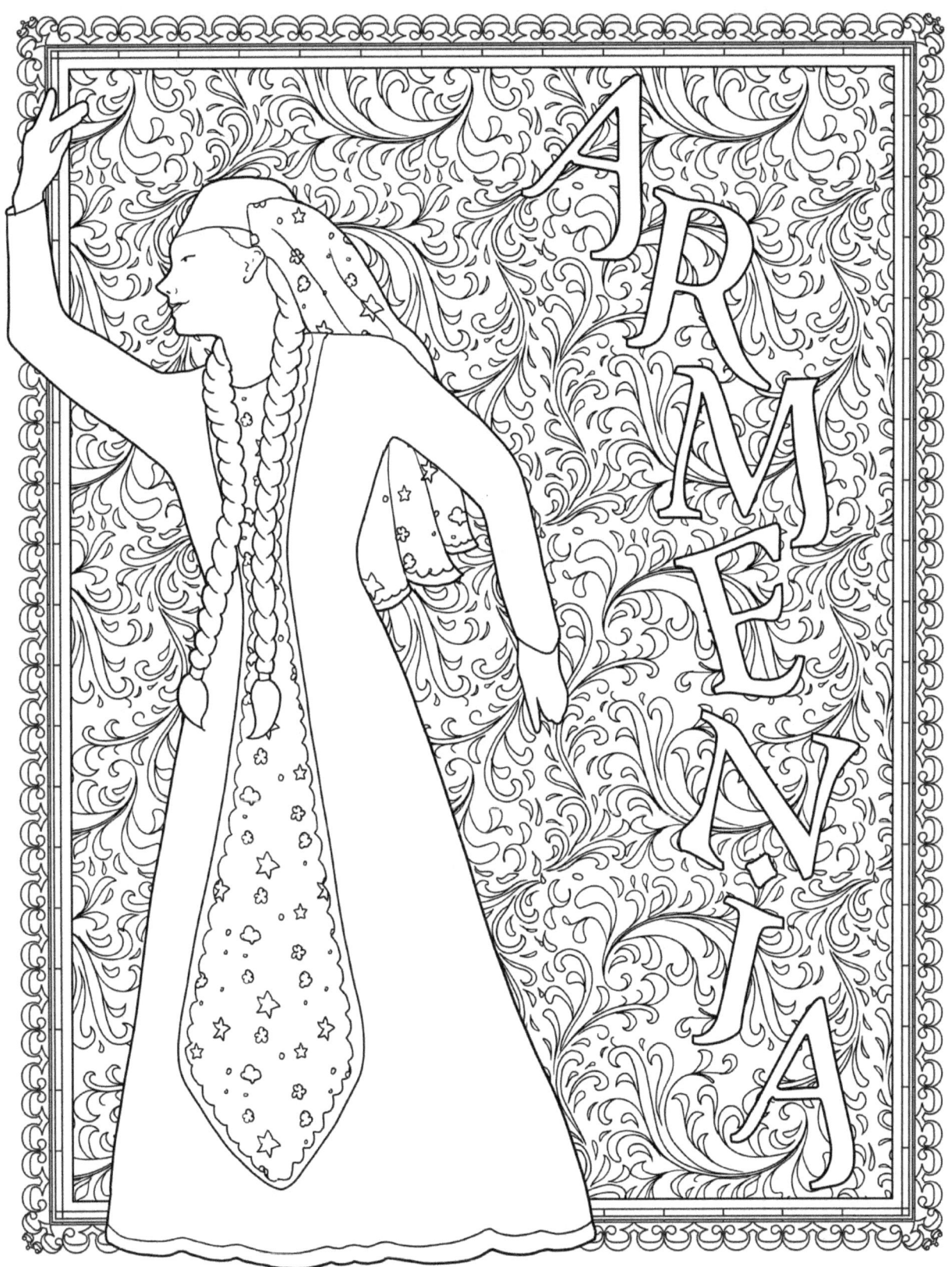

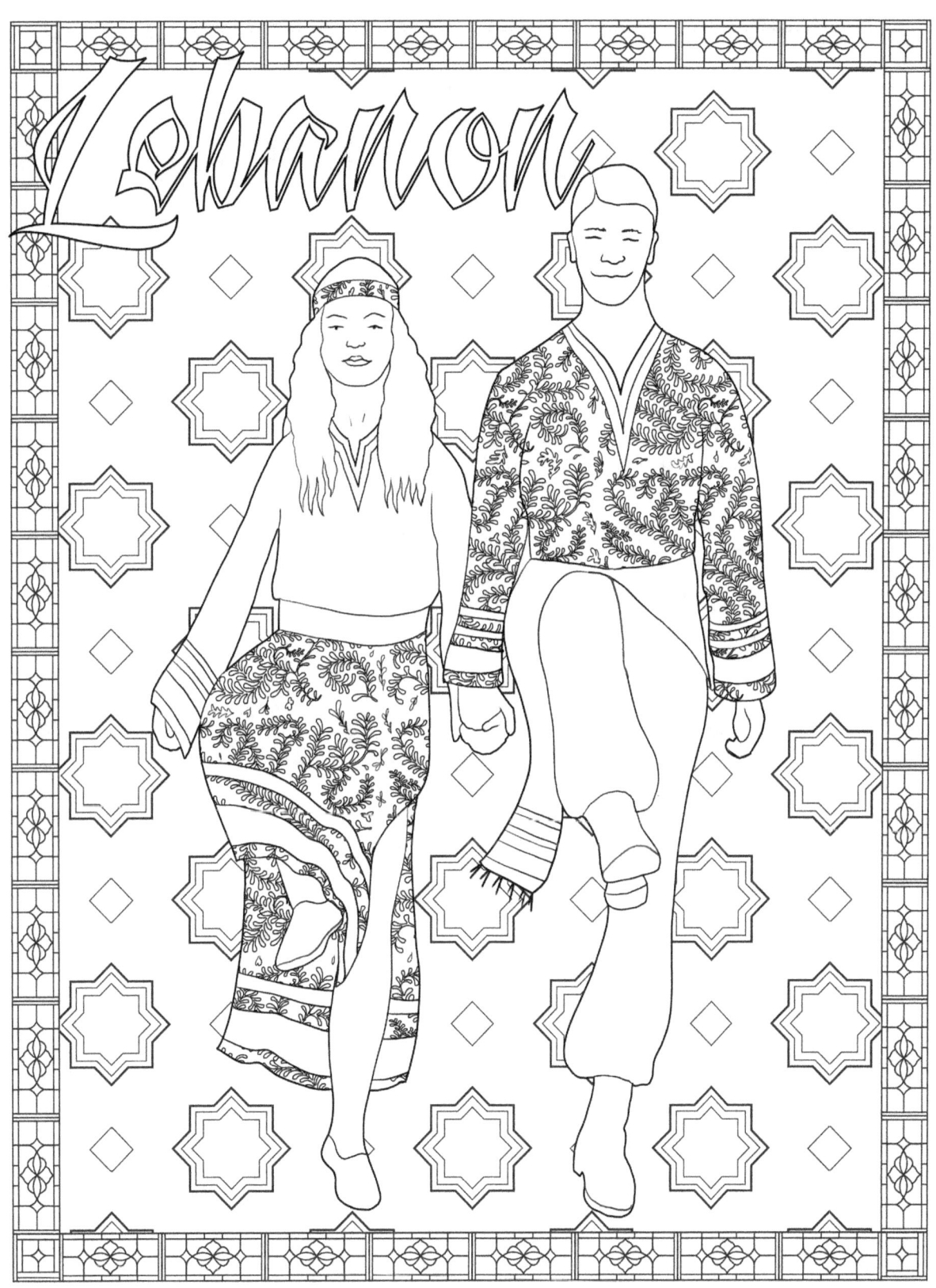

ASIA/PACIFIC

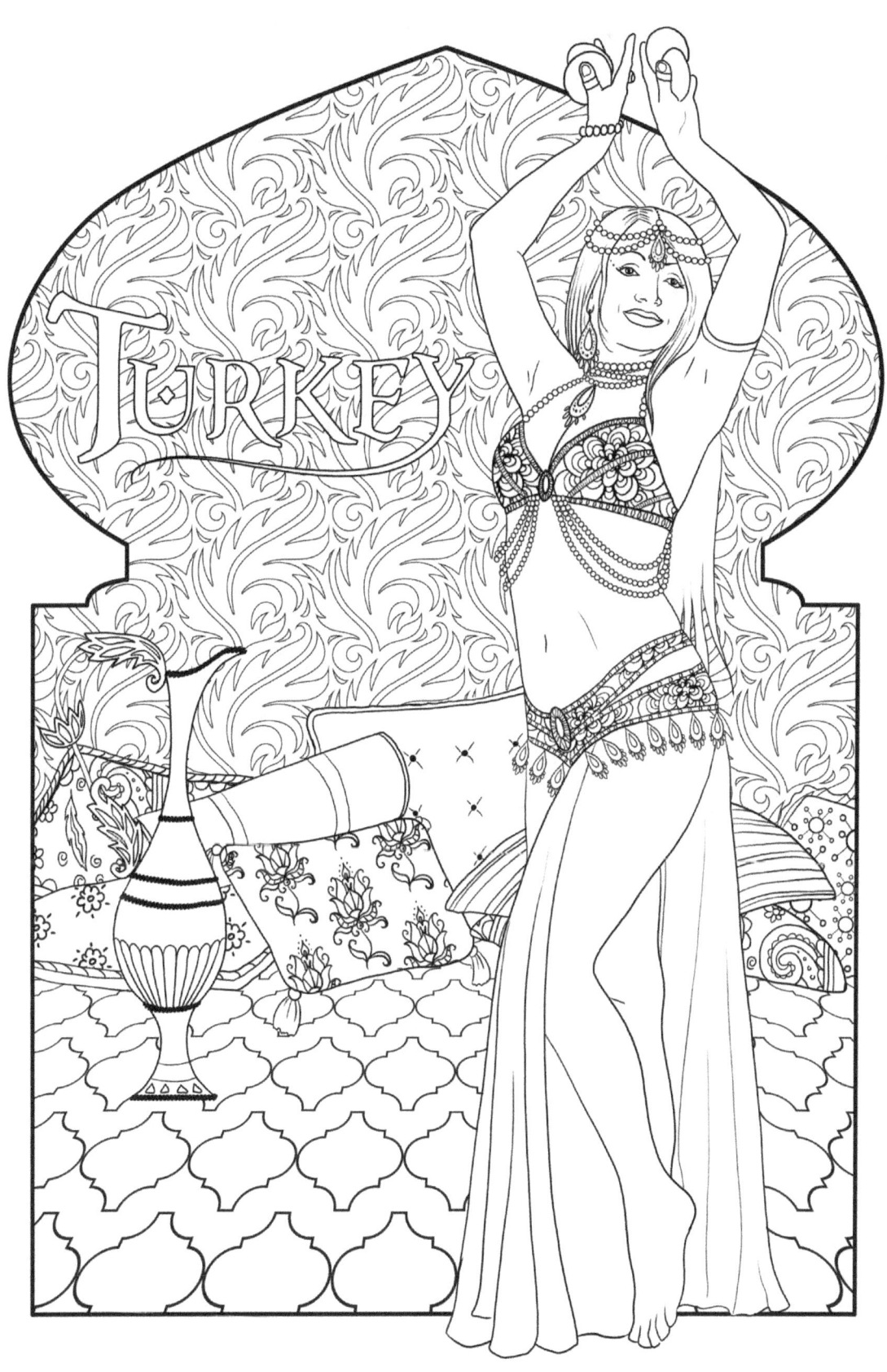

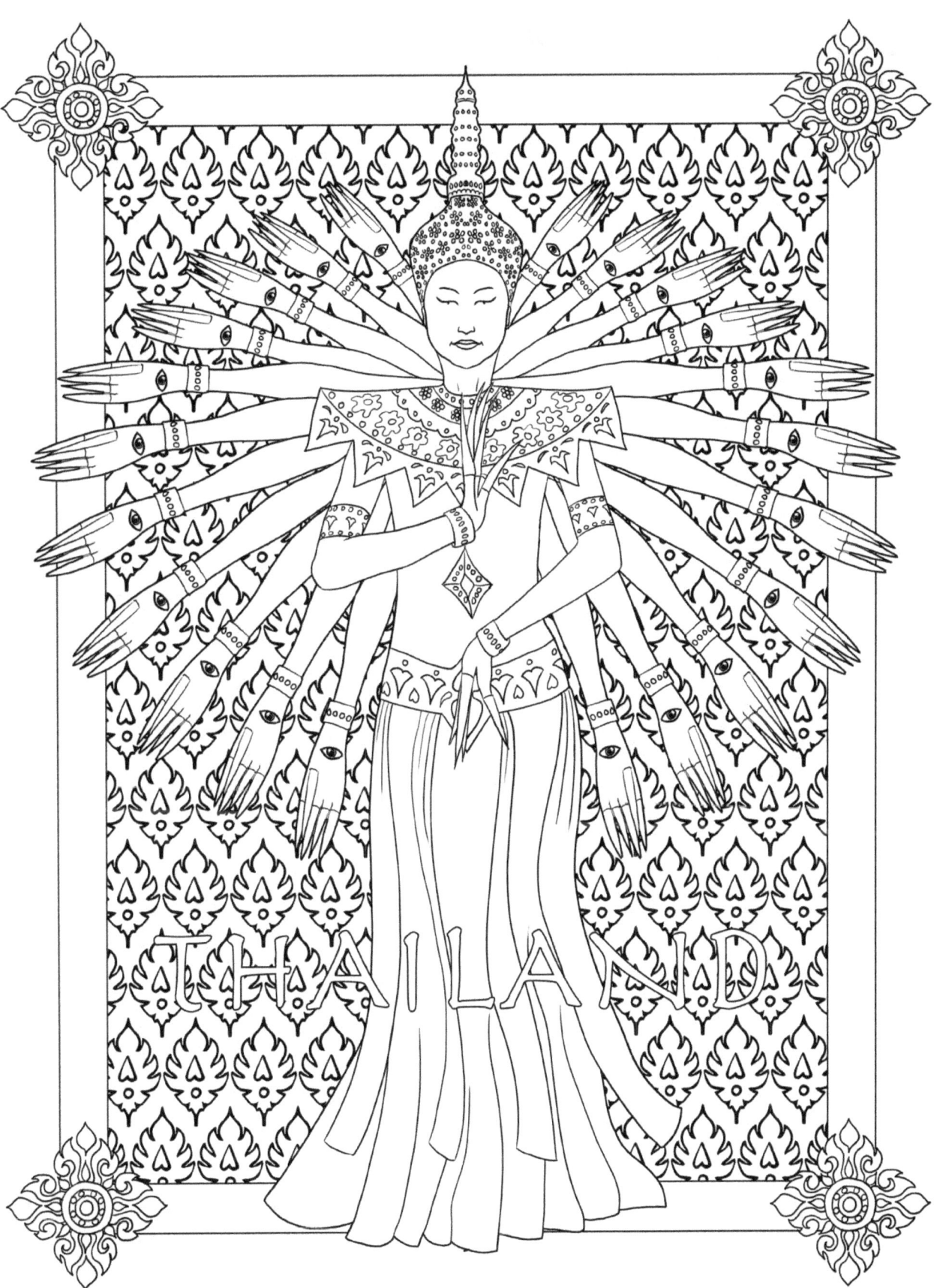

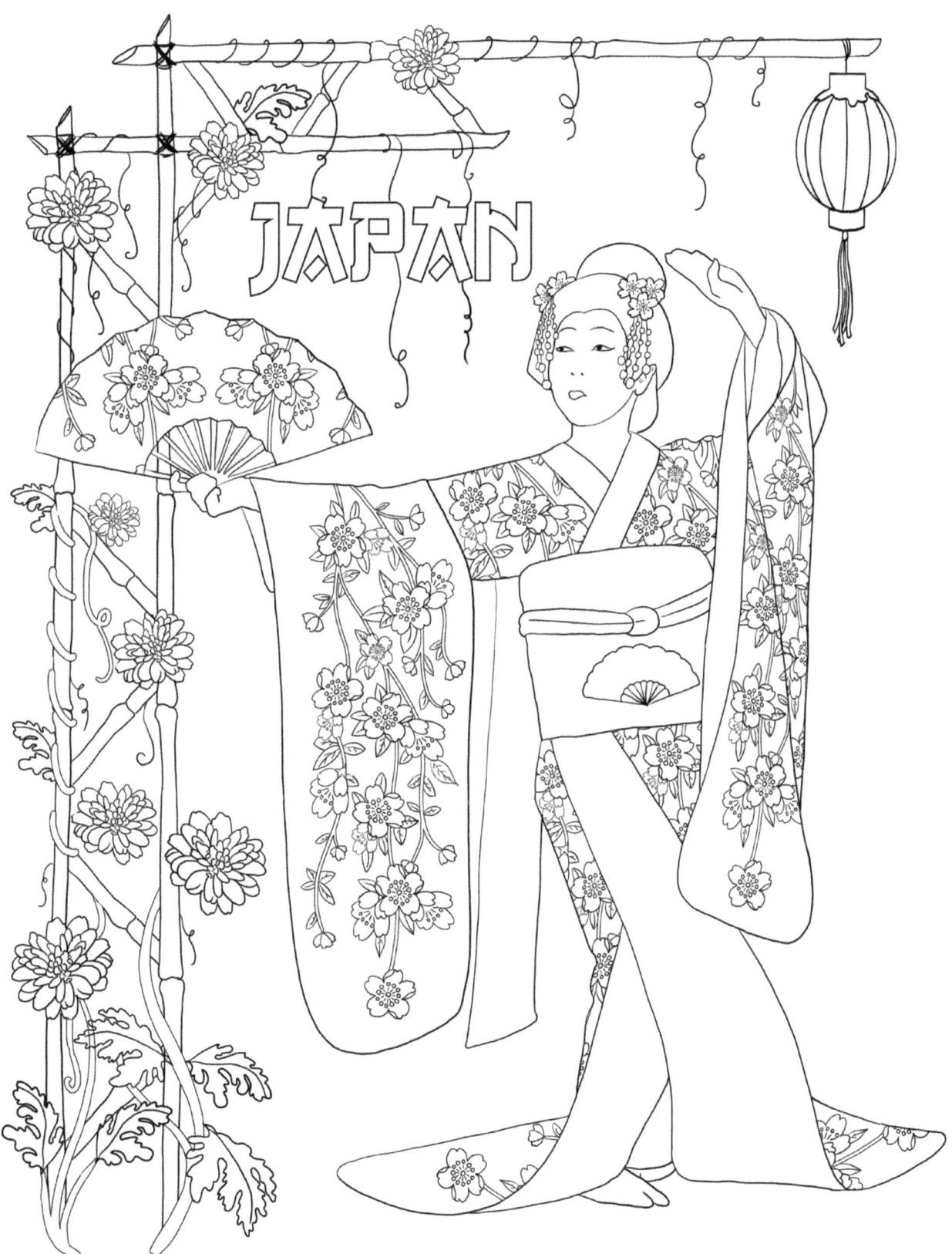

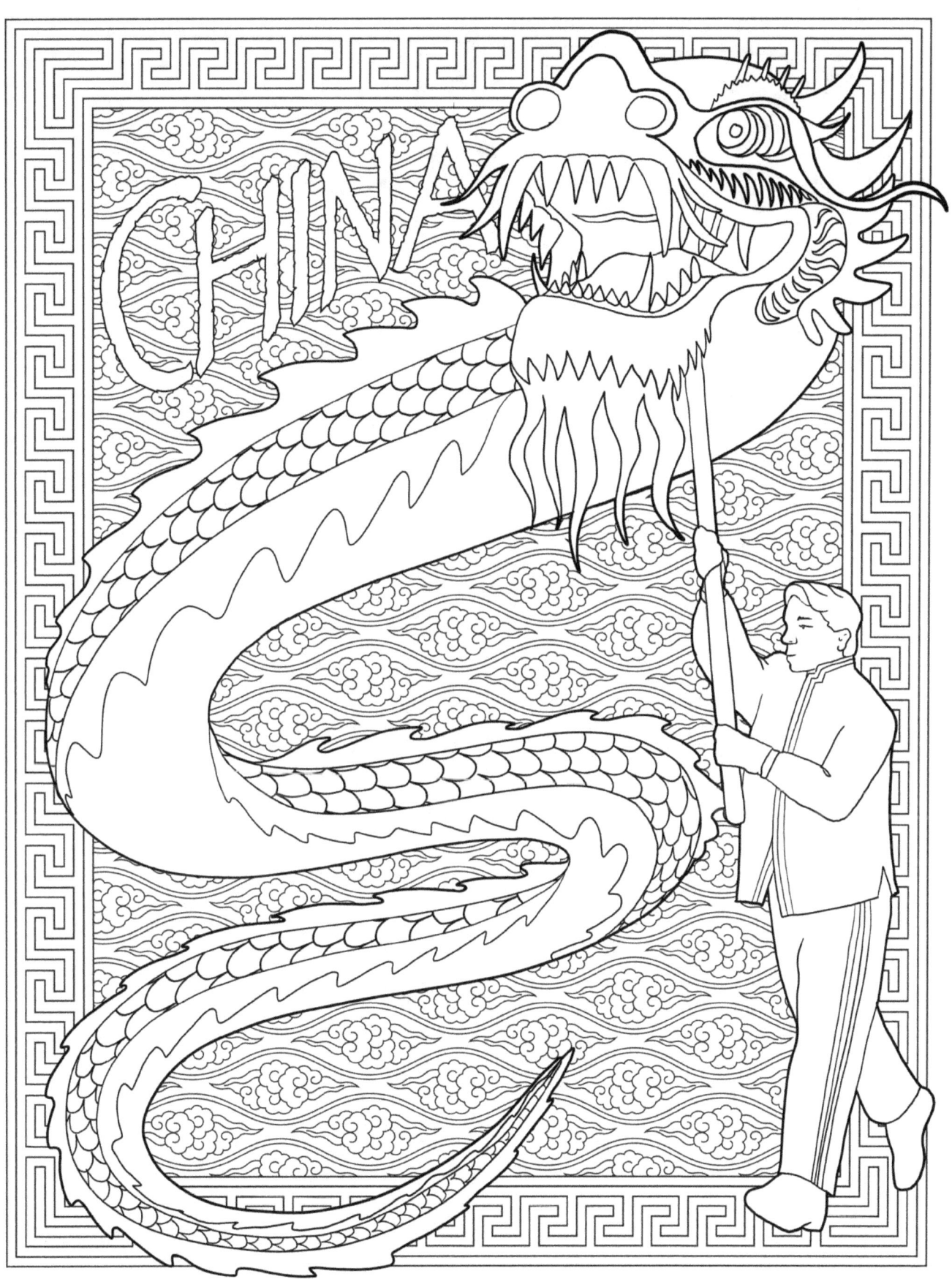

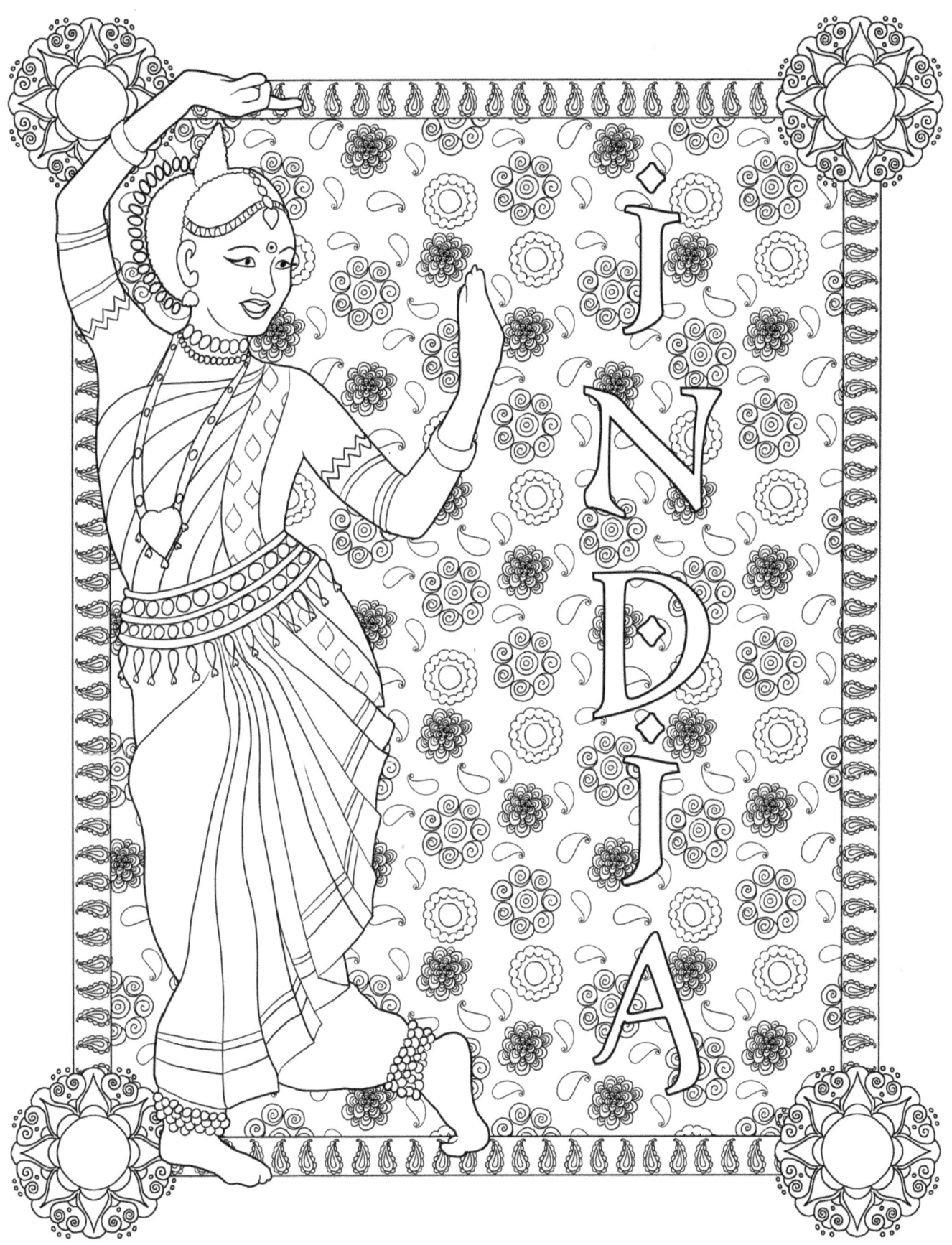

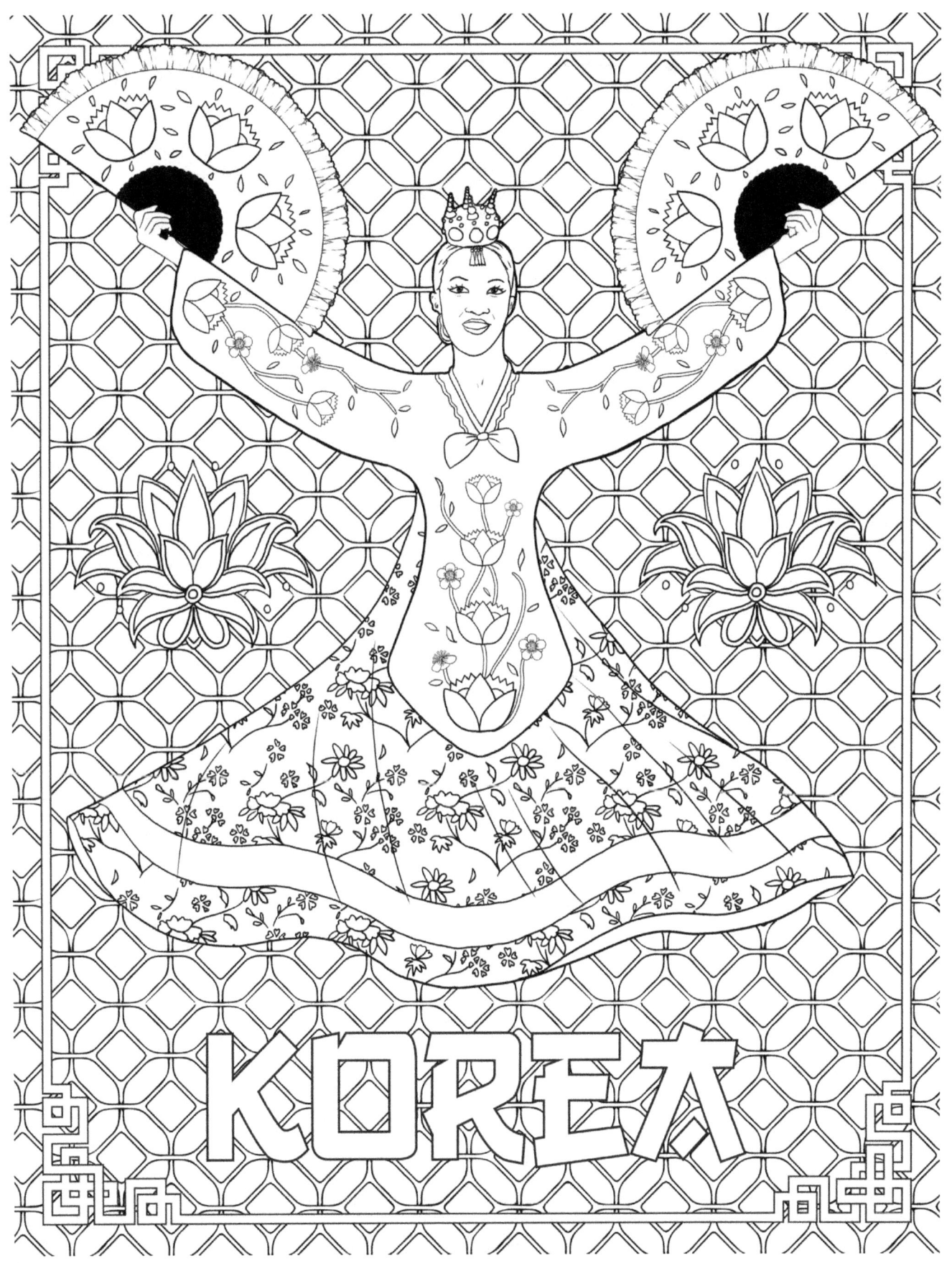

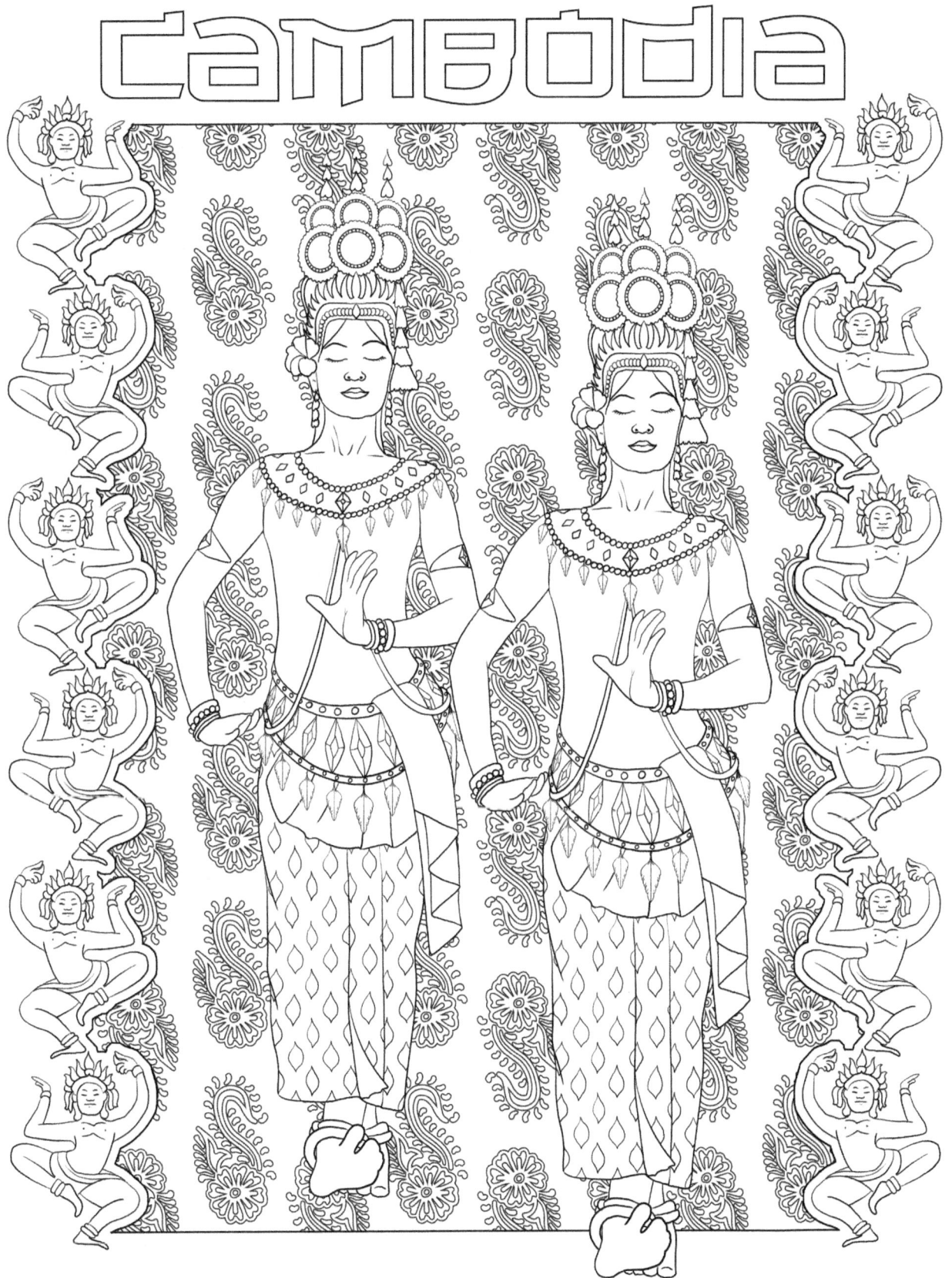

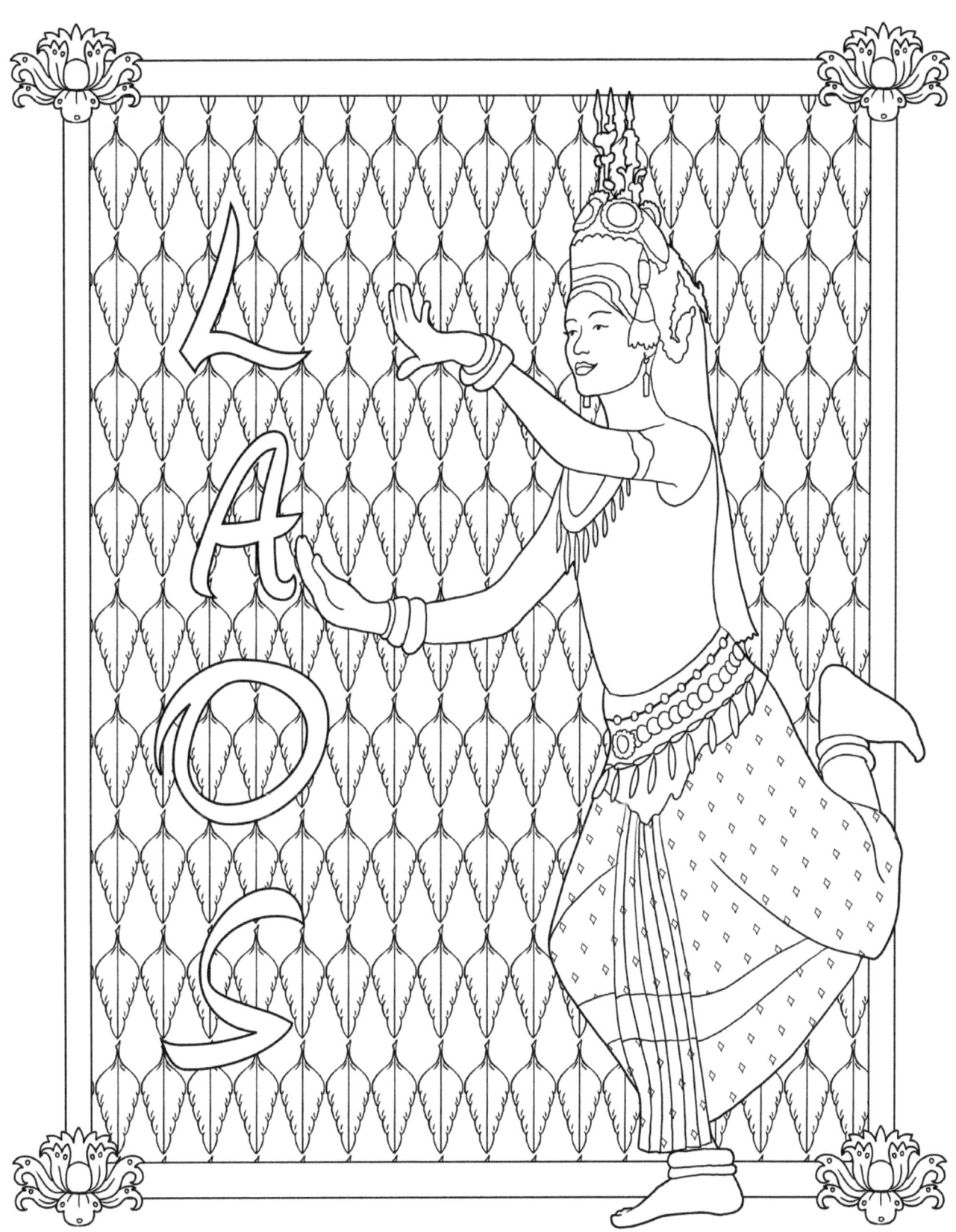

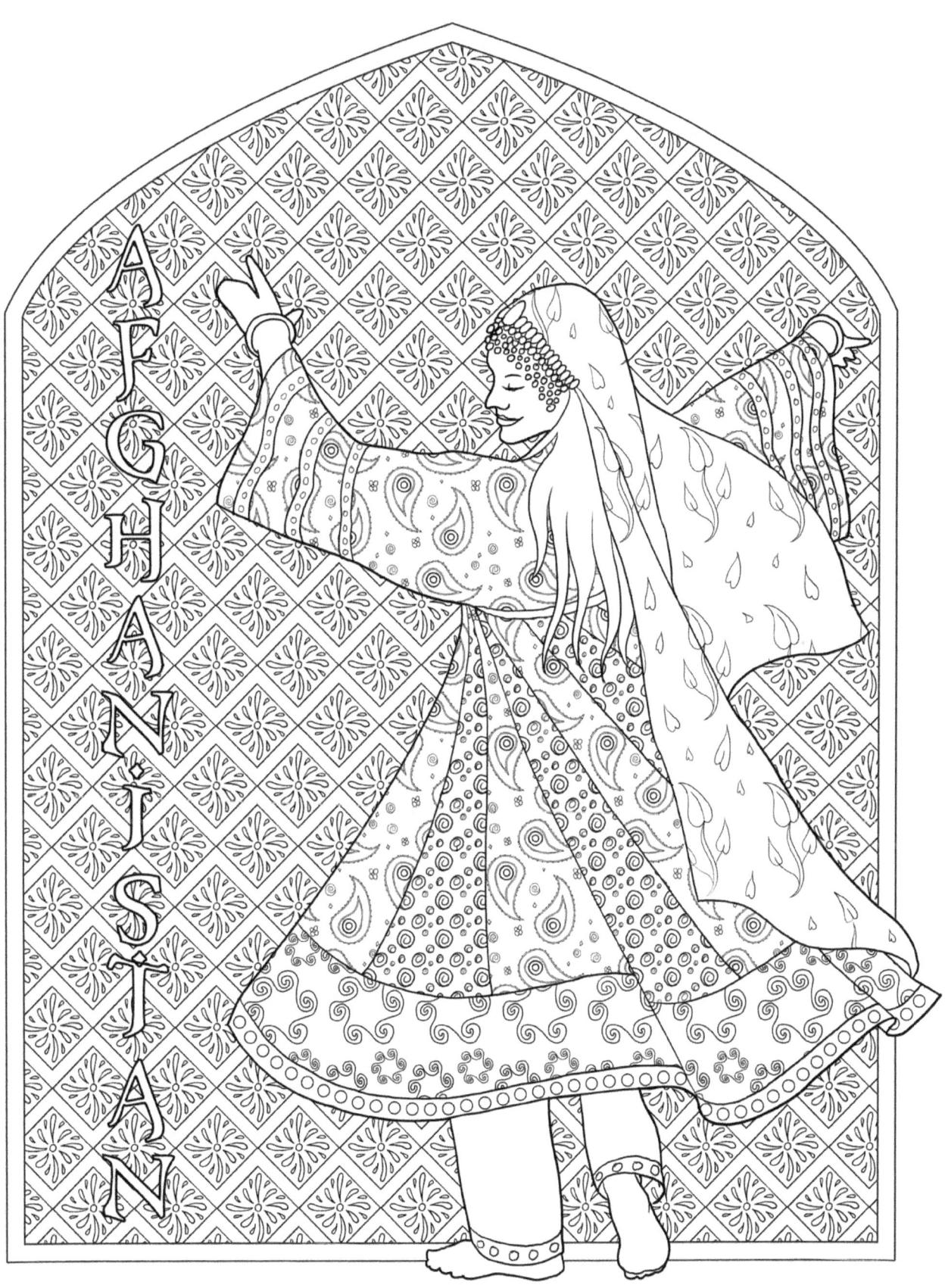

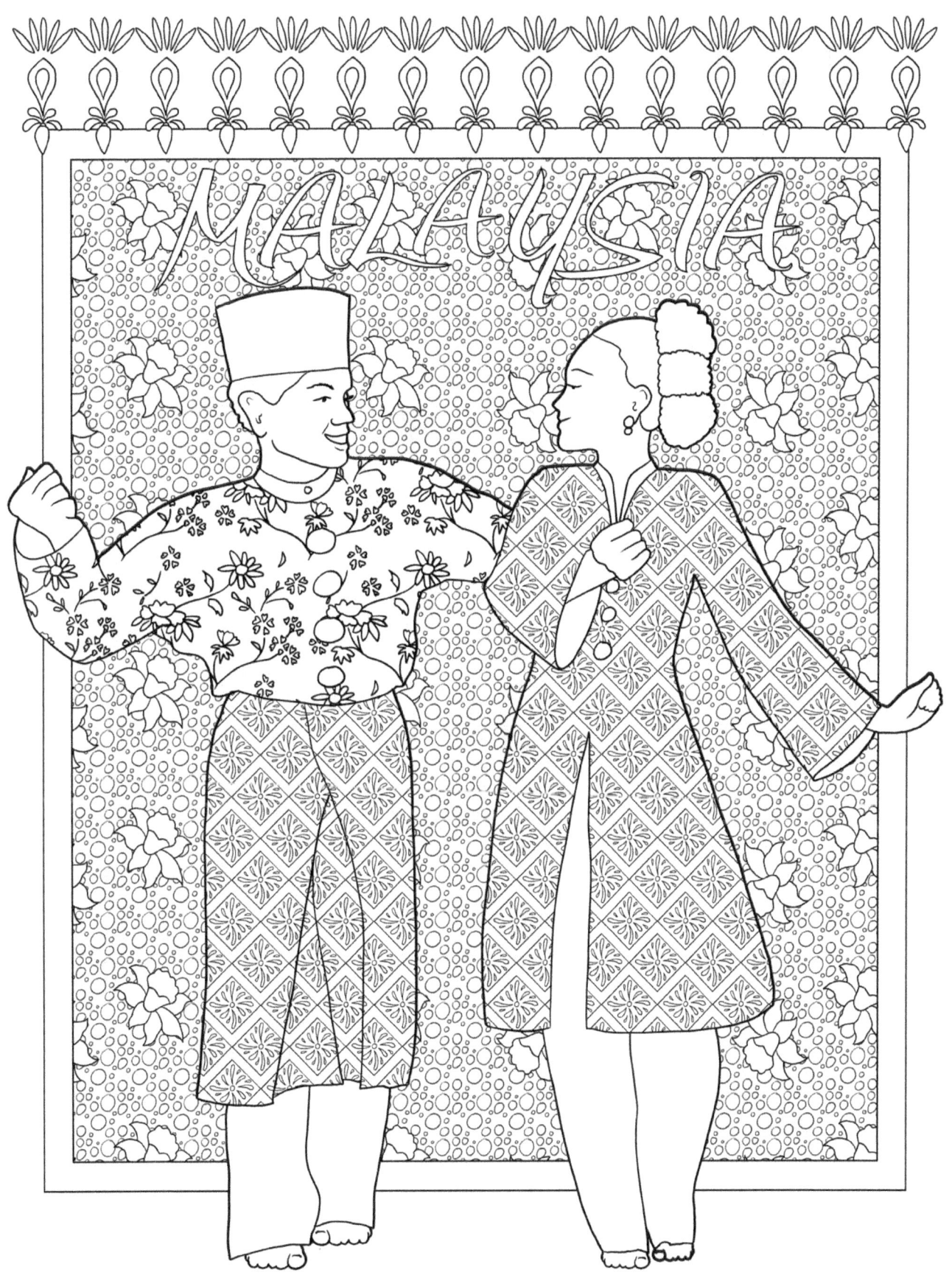

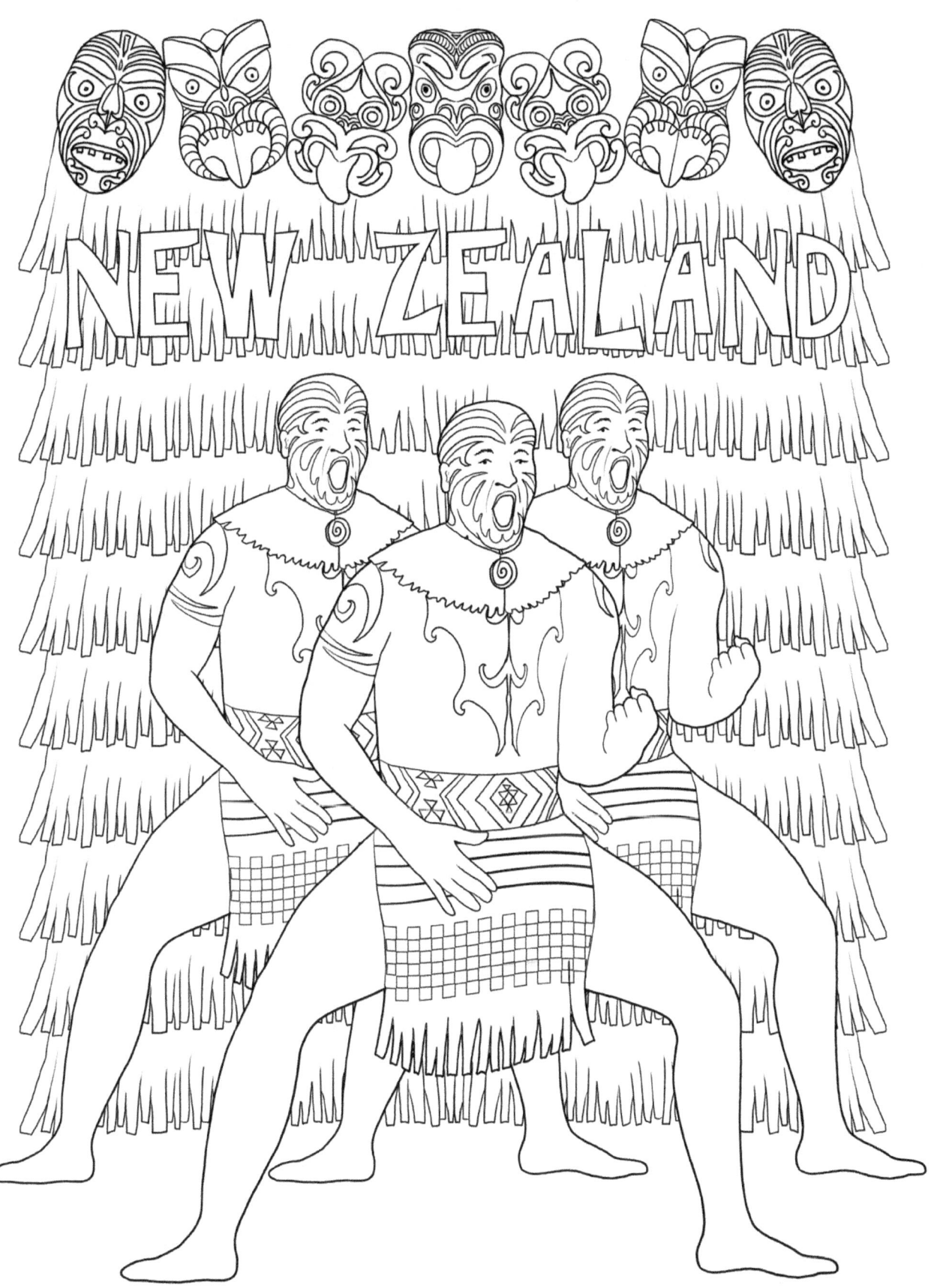

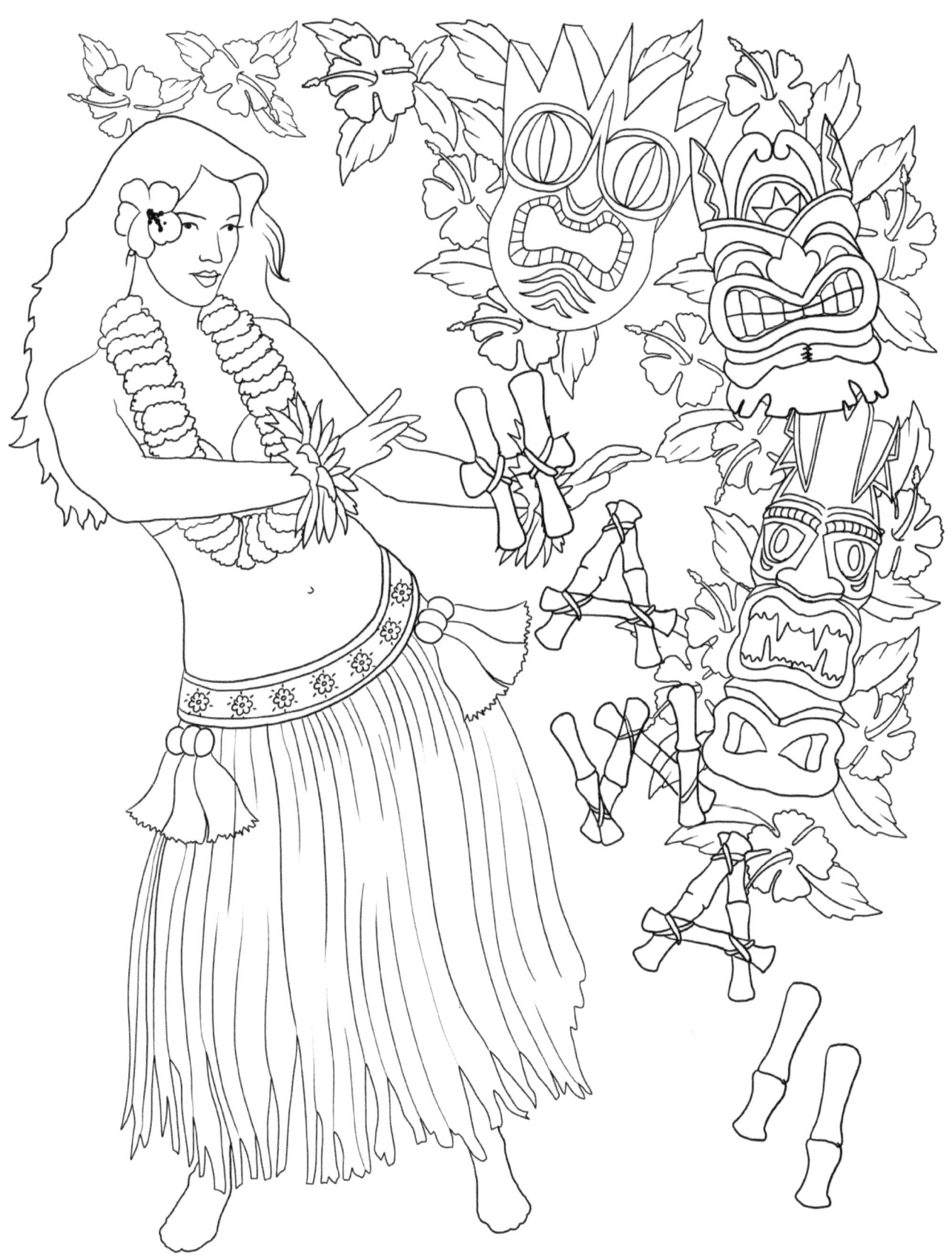

www.ingramcontent.com/pod-product-compliance
Lightning Source LLC
Chambersburg PA
CBHW080950170526
45158CB00008B/2437